By Lucian Vance

Portions of this book originally appeared in *Bias in the Media* by Hal Marcovitz.

LUCENT
PRESS

302.23
VAN

Published in 2018 by
Lucent Press, an Imprint of Greenhaven Publishing, LLC
353 3rd Avenue
Suite 255
New York, NY 10010

Designer: Seth Hughes
Editor: Jennifer Lombardo

Library of Congress Cataloging-in-Publication Data

Names: Vance, Lucian.
Title: Fake news and media bias / Lucian Vance.
Description: New York : Lucent Press, 2018. | Series: Hot topics | Includes
 bibliographical references and index.
Identifiers: LCCN 2017046663| ISBN 9781534561991 (library bound book) | ISBN
 9781534562912 (pbk. book) | ISBN 9781534562004 (ebook)
Subjects: LCSH: Journalism–Objectivity–United States. | Mass
 media–Objectivity–United States. | Fake news–United States.
Classification: LCC PN4888.O25 V36 2018 | DDC 302.230973–dc23
LC record available at https://lccn.loc.gov/2017046663

Printed in the United States of America

CPSIA compliance information: Batch #CW18KL: For further information contact Greenhaven Publishing LLC, New York,
New York at 1-844-317-7404.

Please visit our website, www.greenhavenpublishing.com. For a free color catalog of all our
high-quality books, call toll free 1-844-317-7404 or fax 1-844-317-7405.

CONTENTS

Adolescence is a time when many people begin to take notice of the world around them. News channels, blogs, and talk radio shows are constantly promoting one view or another; very few are unbiased. Young people also hear conflicting information from parents, friends, teachers, and acquaintances. Often, they will hear only one side of an issue or be given flawed information. People who are trying to support a particular viewpoint may cite inaccurate facts and statistics on their blogs, and news programs present many conflicting views of important issues in our society. In a world where it seems everyone has a platform to share their thoughts, it can be difficult to find unbiased, accurate information about important issues.

It is not only facts that are important. In blog posts, in comments on online videos, and on talk shows, people will share opinions that are not necessarily true or false, but can still have a strong impact. For example, many young people struggle with their body image. Seeing or hearing negative comments about particular body types online can have a huge effect on the way someone views himself or herself and may lead to depression and anxiety. Although it is important not to keep information hidden from young people under the guise of protecting them, it is equally important to offer encouragement on issues that affect their mental health.

The titles in the Hot Topics series provide readers with different viewpoints on important issues in today's society. Many of these issues, such as teen pregnancy and Internet safety, are of immediate concern to young people. This series aims to give readers factual context on these crucial topics in a way that lets them form their own opinions. The facts presented throughout also serve to empower readers to help themselves or support people they know who are struggling with many of the challenges adolescents face today. Although negative viewpoints are not ignored or downplayed, this series allows young people to see that the challenges they face are not insurmountable. Eating disorders can be overcome, the Internet can be navigated safely, and pregnant teens do not have to feel hopeless.

Quotes encompassing all viewpoints are presented and cited so readers can trace them back to their original source, verifying for themselves whether the information comes from a reputable place. Additional books and websites are listed, giving readers a starting point from which to continue their own research. Chapter questions encourage discussion, allowing young people to hear and understand their classmates' points of view as they further solidify their own. Full-color photographs and enlightening charts provide a deeper understanding of the topics at hand. All of these features augment the informative text, helping young people understand the world they live in and formulate their own opinions concerning the best way they can improve it.

History of Media Bias

The news media is one of the most important parts of a free society. Their duty is to tell the truth to help people understand what is happening in the world around them and make informed decisions. When journalists allow their own personal biases to affect the way they report the news, they hurt their viewers by spreading misinformation that is incorrect at best and dangerous at worst.

Adding to the media bias problem is the issue of fake news, which has been gaining more attention since the 2016 presidential election. As the Internet has become an ever-present part of 21st-century life, it has become more difficult to take things online at face value. One popular meme pokes fun at this phenomenon by attributing a quote, "The problem with quotes on the Internet is that it is hard to verify their authenticity," to Abraham Lincoln. Sometimes the meme is accompanied by a picture of Benjamin Franklin, implying that he is Lincoln. This meme points out that just because something can be found online does not make it true.

People often use incorrect facts and misleading photos to influence the opinions of others, and if they do their job well enough, they can sometimes even affect things such as the way people cast their votes for certain candidates or policies. Thinking critically about information is more important than ever in an age where anyone with an Internet connection can present their opinions as fact without providing any kind of proof.

The Spread of Bias

Hundreds of American newspapers, magazines, and other publications, as well as numerous television and radio shows, are devoted to news and commentary. The growth of the Internet has provided opportunities for almost anyone in the world to reach audiences that have often totaled in the millions. Tens of thousands of blogs report news and commentary, and these are available to anyone with Internet access. There is no dedicated person or group watching what news outlets print; the U.S. government has no role in ensuring that stories appearing in the press are unbiased. Therefore, it is up to the media themselves to decide whether their presentations of the news are biased. In some cases, when readers or critics point out cases of bias, news organizations are quick to respond and correct the record.

Bias can emerge in several ways. One reason for biased reporting is to attract viewers who hold a certain viewpoint. For instance, Fox News tends to attract conservative viewers, while CNN tends to attract liberal viewers. Other news outlets and blogs are generally also slanted in one direction or another— some much more than others. Another reason for bias is that journalists and media owners use their power over the press to promote political leaders and the policies they favor. Sometimes bias can be very subtle. A journalist may develop a preconceived notion of how a story should be told before they conduct the first interviews. When this happens, the reporter will generally seek out interviewees who can be counted on to provide comments that will be in agreement with the way the journalist sees the story. Sometimes bias even happens unintentionally. Many people, even reporters, believe the news should be unbiased. However, as reporter Timothy Stanley wrote in an article for CNN, "The press is staffed by human beings, and those human beings have prejudices conditioned by race, class, gender and religion."[1]

Consequences of Bias and Fake News

Media bias is not a new problem. In 2001, a series of race riots erupted in Cincinnati, Ohio, after a white police officer shot an unarmed black man. White readers of the *Cincinnati Enquirer* newspaper were truly shocked when they read the stories about the rioting; they could not figure out why black people were so angry about this one incident. What they did not know was that African American community leaders had been complaining about the police for months, stating that black citizens had been abused and harassed by white police officers.

Many white people in Cincinnati were unaware of police brutality in the black community before 2001, since it often was not reported. The issue was not addressed by the Cincinnati Enquirer *until rioters took to the streets and made themselves heard.*

White readers of the *Enquirer* were not aware of the police abuses or the simmering anger in the black community because the newspaper had failed to do its job. Because the *Enquirer* had not assigned reporters to cover the issue more fully and because the mostly white members of the news staff had few sources in the black community, the newspaper's executives and journalists, like everyone else in Cincinnati, were unprepared when the racial unrest erupted into violence. In the months leading up to the rioting, the *Enquirer*'s coverage of racial issues in Cincinnati was biased against the black community. In the *Enquirer*'s case, the newspaper committed bias by neglect—by ignoring the problems in the black community, the newspaper's coverage gave the false impression to its readers that race relations in Cincinnati were healthy and progressive.

Following the riots in Cincinnati, the *Enquirer* took steps to increase understanding of problems in the black community. Along with other community service and education groups, the newspaper helped organize a series of town hall meetings in which members of the community, sociologists, members of the newspaper staff, city political leaders, and others were encouraged to discuss race relations. About 2,100 people participated in 145 community meetings sponsored by the newspaper. Following the meetings, the *Enquirer* used its editorial, or opinion, pages to urge the city to rehabilitate impoverished neighborhoods rather than commit its resources to upscale shopping districts. *Enquirer* editorials also urged Cincinnati school administrators to add courses on racial tolerance to the curricula of city schools. The newspaper even provided resources to Cincinnati teachers to help them talk about racism in their classes, creating a database on its website of stories and reports about racial issues. The paper did many things to correct its mistake, but unfortunately, this rarely happens in other instances of media bias.

Although media bias has been around as long as there have been news outlets, the term "fake news" has increasingly been used since the 2016 U.S. presidential election. This generally refers to stories that are outright lies. However, the term is not always used accurately. Some stories that are labeled fake news are indeed completely made up, but it is a label that is sometimes used to discredit any story with which a person disagrees. Both fake news and the misuse of the term to describe real news stories can have dangerous consequences.

Where Does Media Bias Come From?

For centuries, societies have come to depend on access to accurate information on current events. On a daily basis, people all around the globe turn to newspapers, television, and the Internet to keep themselves informed. Many people perceive the world through the stories they encounter in the media and make important life decisions based on that understanding. It is no surprise that many self-interested individuals and groups have used the media to shape people's specific political or social opinions.

Understanding media bias is important, but knowing media bias exists can have a dangerous effect. In some cases, people will invent stories and try to give them credibility by claiming that the media is too biased to report them. This can further complicate things; people are aware that the mainstream media does ignore certain stories, but it is nearly impossible to figure out which stories are truly being ignored and which are being promoted by people who want to sway the opinions of others.

Journalistic Standards

Although media bias exists, journalism is a profession that operates under a code of standards and ethics designed largely to ensure that bias does not color the news. Many news organizations try to follow certain standards of good journalism that have evolved over the course of more than two centuries. This code of ethics is not law, and there is no formal punishment for not following it. A news source that is reputable, or trustworthy, will follow this code because the reporters believe it is the right thing to do.

Defining Political Views

Journalists are often accused of having a liberal or conservative bias. The two ideologies, or beliefs, form the basis for most mainstream political thought in America today. Each ideology traces its roots back hundreds of years to the emergence of democracy in Europe, when liberals advocated swift and decisive change while conservatives preached caution and gradual change.

Today, liberalism and conservatism have been refined to fit into the confines of American society. According to Geoffrey R. Stone, a law professor at the University of Chicago, liberals question authority but remain respectful of different opinions. He says liberals look to government to protect individual liberties. Stone wrote, "It is liberals who maintain that a national community is like a family and that government exists in part to 'promote the general welfare.'"[1]

Modern conservatives also stand for individual freedoms, but they maintain that government should play a limited role in society. According to conservative editor Donald J. Devine, conservatives value the strength provided by traditional institutions, such as church, family, business, local communities, and national patriotism. "Freedom and markets cannot exist without a traditional, even religious, social order to sustain them," Devine wrote. "The state is often the greatest threat to traditional values and institutions."[2]

1. Geoffrey R. Stone, "Liberal Values," *Huffington Post*, updated May 25, 2011. www.huffingtonpost.com/geoffrey-r-stone/liberal-values_b_31218.html.

2. Dr. Donald J. Devine, "Freedom and Tradition: Why We Are Conservative," The American Conservative Union, accessed October 4, 2017. conservative.org/found-conservatism/freedom-tradition/.

In most cases, individual newspapers, TV networks, and other news outlets have developed their own rules and ethical standards so their reporters and editors know what is expected of them as they report the news. The *New York Times*, for example, has a guide issued to its reporters and editors specifying that they have a responsibility to remain impartial observers at news events, that they are not permitted to receive money or gifts from the people or organizations they cover, and that they must not enter into romantic relationships with the people they cover. In addition, sports writers are prohibited from gambling on sporting events, movie critics may not invest in films that are in production, and travel writers may not accept free trips from tour promoters. These rules are designed to ensure that the newspaper or website remains trustworthy and neutral—for instance, if a sports writer loses a bet on a team they are covering, the sportswriter may take out their grudge on the team in print; or if a movie critic has invested in a film, that critic's review of the film will undoubtedly be positive, regardless of how good or bad the film may be. The *Times*'s policy on ethics in journalism states, "The core purpose of The New York Times is to enhance society by creating, collecting and distributing high-quality news and information. Producing content of the highest quality and integrity is the basis for our reputation and the means by which we fulfill the public trust and our customers' expectations."[2]

Journalists in TV and print media should report only the facts. Rules and ethical expectations help journalists remain impartial and prevent them from interfering in events.

OBJECTIVE AND INDEPENDENT

"Our greatest accomplishment as a profession is the development since World War II of a news reporting craft that is truly non-partisan, and non-ideological, and that strives to be independent of undue commercial or governmental influence."

—Howell Raines, former executive editor of the *New York Times*

Quoted in Tim Groseclose and Jeffrey Milyo, "A Measure of Media Bias," *Quarterly Journal of Economics*, November 2005, p. 1,192.

The ethical standards under which most news organizations operate are similar. In 2001, the Washington, D.C.–based journalism advocacy group Pew Research Center's Project for Excellence in Journalism boiled these ethics down to a set of nine principles. These guidelines are designed to guide the media and ensure a fair and unbiased presentation of the news. These principles are:

- The first obligation of the journalist is to tell the truth.

- A journalist's first loyalty is to the citizens.

- All information presented in a news story must be verifiable as fact.

- Journalists must maintain independence from those they cover.

- Journalism must be an independent monitor of power.

- Journalism must be a forum for criticism.

- Journalism must provide information that is relevant to people's lives.

- Journalists must keep the news in proper perspective, not inflating the importance of minor issues or minimizing the significance of major developments.

- Journalists must possess a conscience and moral compass.

In a perfect world, journalists and editors as well as the people who own newspapers, TV networks, radio stations, and websites would adhere to these principles. In fact, though, violations of the Pew principles occur regularly.

Are Editorials Biased Reporting?

One important part of the media is sections that discuss the reporters' opinions. These are called editorials because they are generally written by editors. Because they are very clearly labeled as an opinion, not fact, they are not considered to be part of an organization's bias. Editorials are important because they give people different perspectives based on the facts of a matter, allowing them to consider angles they may never have thought of before.

Editorials fulfill roles outlined in the Pew Research Center's principles: providing forums for criticisms and ideas, serving as monitors on those in power, keeping the news in perspective, and always using facts to make their case.

Publications have opinion columns that are still able to remain free of bias in their actual reporting. Such columns reflect the opinion of the author, not the organization as a whole.

When people read a newspaper's editorials or opinion columns, they are well aware that what they are reading is opinion, and if the publication is credible, they know those commentaries are grounded in facts and that the writers are not twisting those facts for deceptive purposes. The simple fact that those columnists and editorial writers are expressing opinions does not make them biased; rather, they are providing readers and viewers with ideas based on reason. Mike Argento, a columnist for the *York Daily Record* in Pennsylvania and former president of the National Society of Newspaper Columnists, wrote, "Our job isn't to report rumors or throw out opinions that are not based on fact or to report opinions as fact. Our job is to commit journalism."[3]

Trust and Confidence
by Americans in Mass Media

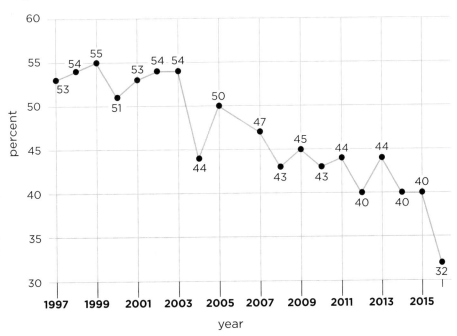

According to this information from a Gallup poll, a record low number of Americans trusted the media in 2016.

The News Business

Many news professionals have spent their entire careers following the principles of ethical journalism, but many others have not. The history of the American media is filled with stories of journalists as well as wealthy press barons dictating how their newspapers and broadcast networks should cover and slant the news.

One case involved a man named William Loeb, who established his newspaper, the *Manchester Union Leader*, as a dedicated voice of conservatism. The newspaper is located in New Hampshire, which is the site of the first presidential primary and therefore has often played a key role in molding public opinion for or against presidential candidates of both parties. In early 1972, just days before the state's presidential primary, the *Union Leader* published a letter from a Florida man on its front page that accused presidential candidate Edmund Muskie of using the word "Canuck" to refer to Americans of French Canadian ancestry. This group of Americans just happens to make up a large proportion of the New Hampshire voters. In this context, Canuck was interpreted to be an insult, even though it is sometimes used as a friendly nickname in other contexts, such as the name of the Canadian hockey team the Vancouver Canucks.

Muskie, at the time the Democratic front-runner for the nomination, became so upset by the charges in the so-called Canuck Letter, as well as other personal attacks leveled at him on the pages of the *Union Leader*, that he called a press conference to denounce the paper and its publisher. In the midst of the press conference, he broke down in tears. The incident helped undermine Muskie's credibility as a candidate; the president is often criticized and insulted in

William Loeb, shown here, founded the Manchester Union Leader *as a way to promote conservatism. He discarded journalistic principles to forward his goal and sabotaged a presidential candidate.*

the press, sometimes in ways that are unfair, and voters tend to lose confidence in a candidate who is unable to handle this aspect of the job. Muskie's breakdown led to his eventual withdrawal from the presidential race. Later, it was revealed that the letter was written by Ken Clawson, a member of the White House staff under Republican president Richard M. Nixon. Nixon regarded Muskie as the biggest threat to his reelection. Nixon's staff members gave the letter to Loeb, who printed it without questioning who it was truly written by. Loeb wanted to see Nixon win the election because he supported Nixon's views and policies. As such, Loeb was not above using the power of his newspaper to help destroy Muskie's candidacy and ensure Nixon's reelection, even if it was unethical.

Bias is not always political; sometimes it can be used to hurt a person or institution financially. For example, Walter Annenberg built up a media empire that included his hometown newspapers, the *Philadelphia Inquirer* and *Philadelphia Daily News*, as well as *TV Guide* and *Seventeen* magazines and local radio and TV stations. For years, Annenberg would not allow the names of certain newsmakers and celebrities to be published if he did not like them because he did not want to give them publicity. In addition to celebrities, Annenberg also harbored a bias against the Philadelphia Warriors, a professional basketball team, most likely because the Warriors engaged in a rental dispute with Annenberg, who owned the arena where they played their games. In retaliation, Annenberg banned news of the Warriors from his newspapers, refusing to send a sportswriter to cover their games. Soon this lack of publicity for the team hurt the Warriors financially, forcing the team to leave Philadelphia. "There were no game stories, no features, no line scores, no mention in the NBA standings box and promotional ads were rejected," wrote Annenberg's biographer, Christopher Ogden. "Game attendance plummeted."[4]

Although Annenberg's low regard for certain celebrities was likely centered on personal biases, his bias against the Warriors stemmed from his financial dispute with the team. As such, he was willing to resort to using the power of the media he controlled to hurt the team financially and drive it out of the city.

More Than Just the Facts

Newspapers air opinions in a number of ways. For example, most newspapers publish editorials. Typically, the page that features editorials is set aside specifically for that purpose and will be headlined "Editorials" to advise readers they are not reading news stories. Editorials represent the position of the newspaper on issues of public importance. They are written by members of the newspaper staff who do not cover stories or otherwise participate in the news-gathering function of the paper. They do not include bylines, which identify the authors. A newspaper's editorial positions are crafted by members of the paper's editorial board, who meet to discuss the issues and decide how the paper's editorial page should respond. Editorial boards often include senior editors, editorial page staff members, and representatives from the paper's corporate offices. Members of the community are often invited to join editorial boards.

Op-eds were traditionally published on the page opposite the editorial page, which is how they got their name. Op-eds are bylined, meaning the author is identified. They are articles that express the opinions of the writers, who often do not work for the newspaper but are recognized as experts in specific fields, such as politics and law.

Opinion columns, which are also bylined, can appear anywhere in the paper. They are generally written by members of the newspaper staff who are specifically assigned to comment on issues in the news.

Newspapers also publish letters to the editor, expressing the opinions of readers. Most newspapers' websites also invite readers to add their comments at the ends of the articles or through blogs maintained to air public discussion on specific issues.

Reporters and Personal Bias

Loeb and Annenberg violated several principles of fair journalism, but bias is not only shown by the powerful people who run news outlets. Many studies of the American media have uncovered bias at the reporting level, where journalists report their stories in ways that show their own beliefs and preconceived notions of what the story should say even before they have all the facts. This occurs even though college journalism students are taught from the first day of their first freshman-level reporting classes to be unbiased, fair, and accurate in their reporting.

NO REGARD FOR THE TRUTH

"I believe there is probably a more irresponsible newspaper [than the *Manchester Union Leader*] in the United States, but I can't think of it. I believe there is a publisher who has less regard for the truth than William Loeb, but I can't think of his name."

–John F. Kennedy, 35th president of the United States

Quoted in David Broder, *Behind the Front Page*. New York, NY: Simon & Schuster, 1987, p. 34.

A 2005 study by former University of California, Los Angeles (UCLA) political scientist Tim Groseclose and University of Missouri economist Jeffrey Milyo examined the issue of bias in the American media. Groseclose and Milyo used a number of factors in comparing the work of several well-known news organizations, such as the sources they cite and the types of stories they cover. The authors concluded that many of the most popular news outlets in America, including the *New York Times*, CBS Evening News, *Washington Post*, and *USA Today*, would receive glowing grades from Americans for Democratic Action, one of the most liberal advocacy organizations in the United States.

In their study, Groseclose and Milyo did not assess editorials, opinion columns, letters to the editor, or other places where opinions are given—only the content of the publications or on-air time devoted to "straight news" stories. The authors concluded, "Our results show a strong liberal bias."[5] However, other studies have found the opposite result. In 2012, a study by Daniel Quackenbush at Elon University found a strong conservative bias in most major media outlets.

BUSINESS OF LIES

"The business of the [journalist] is to destroy the truth, to lie outright, to pervert, to vilify, to fawn at the feet of [the wealthy], and to sell his country and his race for his daily bread. You know it and I know it, and what folly is this toasting an independent press?"

–John Swinton, former writer for the *New York Times*

Quoted in "John Swinton on the Independence of the Press," Constitution Society, March 10, 2002. www.constitution.org/pub/swinton_press.htm.

Unfortunately, studies about media bias have some degree of unreliability. Dave D'Alessio, associate professor of communication at the University of Connecticut, has studied media bias for years. He explained the problem with trying to assess media bias in most cases:

> Broadly speaking, I don't trust anybody that says the media are biased because the very nature of bias is that it's a perception—it's something that people see and they base it on what they see. There's something called a hostile media effect. Basically whenever people are engaged in an issue … they see coverage as biased against their perception, no matter what it is.[6]

This does not mean media bias does not exist, it simply means that people who are claiming the media is biased against their own personal view may be ignoring certain facts. For instance, Donald Trump, the 45th president of the United States, has claimed frequently that the media is biased against him and has been quick to declare that negative news articles are "fake news," even when the facts in a story can be proven beyond a doubt. Many of his supporters take this view as well, while in the eyes of many of his opponents, the opposite is true: They tend not to believe anything good about him, even things that can be proven to be true.

Sometimes White House representatives have used creative phrases to try to explain some statements. In a now-famous video clip, Kellyanne Conway, a presidential advisor in the Trump administration, spoke to NBC reporter Chuck Todd about statements made by then–press secretary Sean Spicer. Todd asked Conway about a lie Spicer was caught in, to which Conway responded that Spicer did not lie, he used "alternative facts." Many people were surprised by this and pointed out that there is no such thing as an alternative fact; this phrase was seen as a way of excusing a lie.

ACCURATE AND INFORMATIVE

"While editorialists and commentators are not neutral, the source of their credibility is still their accuracy, intellectual fairness and ability to inform—not their devotion to a certain group or outcome."

—Pew Research Center's Project for Excellence in Journalism

"Principles of Journalism," American Press Association, accessed October 4, 2017. americanpressassociation.com/principles-of-journalism/

Bias That Influences Reporting

Of course, just because reporters regard themselves as liberal or conservative does not mean their reporting is biased. Many reporters do a very good job of being fair and unbiased, but sometimes the bias comes across in subtle ways that the reporter does not realize have added a slant to the story. Groseclose and Milyo cited one story, published in the *Washington Times*—a conservative news organization—reporting an act of Congress that provided $300,000 to restore opera houses in Connecticut, Michigan, and Washington. The average conservative who opposes unnecessary government spending might be angry and consider this a wasteful use of taxpayer money. The story is technically accurate, but Groseclose and Milyo pointed out that the reporter could have provided a fairer and generally unbiased story about the opera house grants if they had also included the fact that $300,000 is a tiny fraction of a federal budget that spends more than $3 trillion a year.

In recent decades, journalism has become dependent on knowledgeable people with a college degree. Statistically, most journalists have liberal backgrounds, but many conservatives work in the field, too.

On the other side, the authors cited a story aired by CBS News about the administration of former President George W. Bush's decision to expand America's reliance on nuclear power as an energy source. While many Democratic and Republican members of Congress agreed that new nuclear power plants were needed to help America establish energy independence, making the United States less dependent on oil from the Middle East, many environmentalists strongly oppose nuclear energy, mostly because of their concerns that disposing of nuclear fuel waste can be environmentally hazardous. To report the story, the CBS correspondent sought the opinion of Daniel Becker, former director of a very liberal environmental group called the Sierra Club, who gladly provided a provocative comment. "Switching from coal to nuclear power," Becker said, "is like giving up smoking and taking up crack."[7] Although Becker may have accurately reflected his organization's heartfelt opposition to nuclear energy, Groseclose and Milyo found the comment to be particularly incendiary and guaranteed to stoke the passions of liberals. Groseclose and Milyo blamed the correspondent. "These statements," they wrote, "are more an indication of the author's preferences than a fact or prediction."[8]

Even though it faces accusations of bias, there is no question the press continues to serve an important role in American society. Reporters have enabled readers and viewers to witness events in other countries up close. They have provided information on riveting events to readers and viewers eager and anxious for details: assassinations of presidents, the terrorist attacks of September 11, 2001, and the devastation of hurricanes and other disasters. Reporters keep people up to date on important events that affect their lives, such as presidential scandals, potentially dangerous situations, and economic trends. As journalist Kara Hackett wrote, "The real question is not a matter of whether our news is biased or not. It's more about the degree to which reporters make an effort to present an educated, well-researched account of what's going on. And as we know from our history books, while the facts are indisputable, they can look differently to different people."[9] When journalists do their job right, the media can influence society and act as a catalyst for social change. However, when reporters and news executives permit their biases to affect the way they do their jobs, journalism can cost a presidential candidate their career, a city its basketball team, and society, as a whole, the truth that only a fair and balanced press can deliver.

While news organizations are generally expected to remain unbiased, invited experts or commentators may make comments that express a bias.

Coverage Bias

An important way in which bias emerges is the style in which news outlets choose to report on events. In an era where ratings and advertising are important considerations for the news media, an engaging story is essential. The news is not just a means of spreading information, it is also a source of income for its operators.

This bias has become very apparent in recent presidential primaries and elections. If voters are to make a decision about who to elect, they need to be well informed of a candidate's policies, experience, and leadership qualities. However, a report from the Harvard Kennedy School's Shorenstein Center on Media, Politics and Public Policy found that during the 2016 primary elections, only 11 percent of media coverage focused on the candidates' actual qualifications.

Instead of essential information, reporting focused heavily on the "horse race"—stories about which candidates were winning and losing. These reports were devoted to poll results, delegates won, amount of money raised, and strategy used by the candidates during the primary process. The results of early elections strongly influenced how the news depicted a candidate, as "leading" or "losing," and focused on their ability to win small contests rather than their ability to be president. This also led to more positive coverage for a candidate with a lead in votes and negative coverage for candidates trailing behind.

While many agree that there should be better reporting of an event with such far-reaching consequences, the nature of presidential campaigns makes it difficult to avoid the horse race style of reporting. The nomination process is long and involves the entire country. Journalists feel obligated to report on things that feel fresh and interesting. A candidate's policy and background do not change on a day-to-day basis, but the actions they take in the election do. When a candidate's policies were reported, journalists were generally discussing how those policies could help or hurt the candidate in a particular contest. Detailed conversations about the issues are much less frequent.

The reporting of candidates has an undeniable impact on how voters make their decisions. A candidate who is winning will generally enjoy coverage centering on why they are winning and depicting a positive image of the candidate. A candidate who is trailing behind will have their negative traits showcased as well as all the obstacles they have to overcome. Early victories in a long contest strongly affect how a candidate is seen for the rest of the nomination process, and voters are responsive to the media portrayal of a person. When it comes time for a voter to decide, they often only have access to information about how a candidate has been succeeding or failing in the election process, rather than a useful discussion of their abilities. It is not until after the primary process is over that a meaningful conversation of the candidates' qualities enters the news—after the votes have been cast and it is too late for voters to change their minds.

In order to keep a long-running story interesting, journalists have a tendency to focus on more exciting aspects of presidential elections rather than having detailed discussions of the issues.

Cable Entertainment and Fake News

Traditionally, the news was a way for people to keep up to date and informed of events in the world. However, as competition for ratings and revenue has increased, cable news networks have drastically changed their presentation of the news. Rather than a reading of the day's events, cable networks present news in the most dramatic and polarizing manner possible. Polarizing means offering two extreme opinions with very little middle ground and encouraging people to take one position or the other. This makes it difficult for people to work together to solve problems in their country, but it also creates drama that is good for network ratings. The mission to inform has become a mission to entertain.

With this presentation of the news, viewership for cable news networks has dramatically increased over the years. In 2016, Fox News saw a 36 percent increase in its prime time ratings. With an average of 2.4 million viewers every night, Fox News was the 5th most watched network in America as of 2016. In the same time period, CNN saw its prime time ratings increase by 79 percent, and MSNBC increased its ratings by 89 percent.

NO NEED FOR FACTS

"There's a lot of inaccurate and incomplete information out there thanks to talk shows from either the left or the right. Facts often get in the way of a good rant."

–Ben Nelson, former senator of Nebraska

Quoted in Don Walton, "Nelson Slams Talk Show Entertainers," *Lincoln Journal Star*, April 17, 2009. www.journalstar.com/articles/2009/04/18/news/local/doc49e91c36bc9c6379122757.txt.

The Fox News network pioneered a confrontational, biased presentation of the news, which has proven to be very popular with its viewers. As of 2016, it was the 5th most watched network.

History of Cable News

At first, the presentation of news on cable TV resembled the typical news formats found on most local and network broadcasts: Essentially, a news anchor sat behind a desk, reading a straightforward account of the news while airing reports in the field by reporters. That is the format viewers saw in 1980 when CNN, the first cable channel to devote itself entirely to news, aired its first broadcast.

CNN was founded by Ted Turner, a businessman from Atlanta, Georgia, who made his fortune selling advertising space on billboards. Turner was among the first entrepreneurs to realize the potential of cable television. He invested heavily in the cable business, buying TV stations and marketing their programming over the nation's growing cable TV systems. In 1980, he launched CNN, featuring news programming 24 hours a day, 7 days a week. Eventually, Turner sold CNN to Time Warner.

CNN had the cable news universe virtually to itself until 1996, when two competitors debuted: MSNBC and Fox News Channel. MSNBC was established by the NBC network in a joint venture with software maker Microsoft. At first, given the influence of Microsoft, the network's interests were supposed to focus on technological and scientific developments that would be of interest to consumers, such as trends in computer and cell phone technology, but that format was soon dropped in favor of straight news coverage, talk shows, and politically oriented interview shows.

Meanwhile, Fox News was launched by Australian-born news baron Rupert Murdoch, who also owns the newspapers *Wall Street Journal* and *New York Post* as well as several other media properties. Murdoch's first move was to put Roger Ailes in charge of Fox News. Ailes had been associated with conservative causes for many years and served as a media adviser to Republican presidents Richard Nixon, Ronald Reagan, and George H.W. Bush. With Ailes in charge of Fox News, the network soon developed an undeniably conservative slant. Author and media critic Brian C. Anderson said,

> *Watch FOX for just a few hours and you encounter a conservative presence unlike anything on television before 1996. Where CBS and CNN would lead a news item about an impending execution with a candlelight vigil of death penalty protesters, for instance, at FOX "it is [required] that we put in the lead why that person is being executed," senior vice president for news John Moody noted a while back. FOX viewers will see Republican politicians and conservative pundits sought out for meaningful quotations, skepticism voiced about environmentalist doomsaying, pro-life views given airtime, and much else they would never find on other networks.*[10]

Ted Turner (left), founder of CNN, and Rupert Murdoch (right), founder of Fox News, have fundamentally changed the landscape of news and entertainment.

Confrontational Journalism

Despite the arrival of MSNBC and Fox News, CNN was still the ratings leader among the cable news networks, due mostly to the widespread popularity of interviewers such as Larry King, who was the host of a nightly talk show. Each evening, King interviewed newsmakers while taking phone calls from viewers at home. People who tuned in to King's show expecting to see guests break down under intense questioning by the host found themselves disappointed—King generally did not grill his guests with tough questions and mostly kept his personal politics to himself. *Washingtonian* magazine media critic Kim Eisler wrote, "He certainly is a server up of 'softballs,' easy questions that are [shunned by] hard-boiled reporters. And his schmoozy style is more suited to a midnight gabfest than to a news show."[11]

In the fall of 2000, as the country's attention was riveted on the unfolding drama of the disputed presidential election results of George W. Bush and Al Gore, Bill O'Reilly, who was the host of *The O'Reilly Factor* on Fox News, surged past King in the ratings. O'Reilly pioneered a much different type of cable host than King. Confrontational, opinionated, and conservative in his outlook, O'Reilly's aggressive style soon attracted a large and dedicated audience, mainly made up of conservatives.

Bill O'Reilly (right) became popular with viewers who leaned toward the political right, or more conservative end of the political spectrum.

By 2009, O'Reilly was hosting the top-rated show on cable news, watched by about 2.4 million viewers per night. Before O'Reilly's dismissal in 2017, his show maintained high ratings.

O'Reilly routinely confronted guests with tough questions and, if he disagreed with them, was not above referring to them in derogatory terms—for instance, one of his favorite insults was "pinhead." In 2007, journalism professors at Indiana University conducted an analysis of *The O'Reilly Factor* and concluded that in the show's opening segment, in which O'Reilly delivered a commentary, the host used a derogatory term for a person or group every 6.8 seconds. The study found that O'Reilly frequently resorted to insults to make his point. For example, the study pointed out that in the weeks leading up to the 2003 invasion of Iraq by the United States and its allies, O'Reilly was highly critical of the French government for refusing to join the coalition that invaded the Middle Eastern country. On his broadcasts, the report said, O'Reilly referred sarcastically to then–French president Jacques Chirac as "our pal … who dislikes America too much"[12] to join the invasion force. According to Mike Conway, one of the study's authors, "It's obvious he's very big into calling people names, and he's very big into glittering generalities. He's not very subtle. He's going to call people names, or he's going to paint something in a positive [or negative] way, often without any real evidence to support that viewpoint."[13]

REINFORCING A FALSE BELIEF

"Recently we did a story about Hillary Clinton being fed the answers prior to the debate. There was already some low level chatter about that having happened–it was all fake–but that sort of headline gets into the right wing bubble and they run with it."

–Allen Montgomery, founder of fake news website The National Report

Quoted in "The Rise and Rise of Fake News," BBC, November 6, 2016. www.bbc.com/news/blogs-trending-37846860.

Modern News Drama

O'Reilly also regularly sent producers out in the field to stage what are known as ambush interviews. Typically, the producer and a camera crew confront somebody on the street—generally an unsuspecting politician, celebrity, or other newsmaker—shouting questions and demanding answers while waving a microphone in the interview subject's face. In 2009, the *New York Times* estimated that O'Reilly's producers had conducted about 50 ambush interviews over the course of the previous 3 years, and the targets for the most part were either liberal political leaders or others who had been critical of Republicans. "When the subjects don't answer," wrote *New York Times* media critic Brian Stelter, "... the questions become more provocative and emotional."[14] In one case cited by Stelter, O'Reilly sent producer Jesse Watters to Virginia Beach, Virginia, to confront then-mayor Meyera Oberndorf, who had upset O'Reilly by saying undocumented immigrants did not deserve to be deported. The mayor's husband responded to the ambush by attempting to grab the microphone from Watters's hand. The effort failed, and the mayor and her husband hurried off. The fact that Watters could not get the mayor to comment seemed of little concern to the producer—instead, Watters was delighted that the fight had been caught on camera. "This will be great TV,"[15] Watters declared. Ambush interviews are considered by many journalists to be in poor taste, but many viewers find them appealing: According to a 2017 study by polling organization Rasmussen, 48 percent of viewers who watch cable news shows every day said they were most likely to watch Fox News.

Fox has also added other conservative commentators to its lineup, and they have carved out their own styles of interviewing guests and providing opinions on the news. Among them is Sean Hannity, who marked President Barack Obama's 100th day in office by playing a video showing various political leaders fighting among themselves and Obama administration officials admitting mistakes in judgment while ominous music played in the background—all meant to illustrate that the liberal Obama administration had gotten off to a rocky start.

Information Avoidance

Although there is certainly bias in the media, individuals play a role in the spread and persistence of misinformation. Psychologists call this information avoidance—the tendency of humans to believe what they want to believe because it makes them happier or more comfortable. Sometimes this means ignoring certain information, while other times it means seeking out the information that makes people happiest; for instance, by only watching a news channel that aligns with a person's views. Carnegie Mellon University explained why this is a problem:

> Questionable evidence is often treated as credible when it confirms what someone wants to believe—as is the case of discredited research linking vaccines to autism. And evidence that meets the rigorous demands of science is often discounted if it goes against what people want to believe, as illustrated by widespread dismissal of climate change.
>
> Information avoidance can be harmful, for example, when people miss opportunities to treat serious diseases early on or fail to learn about better financial investments that could prepare them for retirement. It also has large societal implications.[1]

The researchers explained that giving people information that contradicts their belief does not work because people will often simply ignore it, and in some cases, being proven wrong will actually strengthen a person's belief that they are correct, especially if the information is presented aggressively. They suggested that it is better for people to "find ways not only to expose people to conflicting information, but to increase people's receptivity to information that challenges what they believe and want to believe."[2]

The popular truTV series *Adam Ruins Everything* discussed this in August 2017. The show, which is intended to show people that things they believe may actually be wrong, aired a segment about what it called "the backfire effect":

> One study found that when people concerned about side effects of the flu shot were informed it was safe, they actually became less willing to get it ... Because when you try to change someone's mind, the other person often feels attacked ... Being proven wrong hurts so much, it often causes a fight or flight response.[3]

This is why people who hold a particular belief that is reinforced by the news they read or watch will often discount contradictory information and see it as evidence of bias, even when this is untrue. A large part of this is people's unwillingness to feel unintelligent or easily tricked.

1. Shilo Rea, "Information Avoidance: How People Select Their Own Reality," Carnegie Mellon University, March 13, 2017. 1. www.cmu.edu/news/stories/archives/2017/march/information-avoidance.html.

2. Quoted in Rhea, "Information Avoidance."

3. "Adam Ruins Everything—Why Proving Someone Wrong Often Backfires," YouTube video, 1:39, posted by truTV, August 24, 2017. www.youtube.com/watch?v=Q8NydsXl32s.

MSNBC: A Liberal Counterpoint

As Fox News Channel's audience expanded, MSNBC was blazing its own path. After dropping its emphasis on technological news, the network started putting together a lineup of liberal commentators that included hosts Keith Olbermann and Rachel Maddow. Each added their own twists and dramatic touches to their commentaries. For example, during the George W. Bush administration, Olbermann featured a nightly spot on his show, *Countdown*, that he named "Bushed." The feature was devoted, he said, to the running scandals of the Bush administration, and in each spot, Olbermann highlighted a different example of what he claimed to be wrongdoing by members of the Republican's administration. As for Maddow, David Zurawik, TV columnist for the *Baltimore Sun*, wrote, "Like Olbermann ... she presents only the news that fits her political viewpoint and agenda."[16]

Rachel Maddow, shown here, generally connects with people on the political left, or more liberal side of the political spectrum.

MSNBC's audience has not grown quite as large as that of Fox. However, as each network's audience has grown, it has not been at the expense of the other's. It is clear that both networks are aiming for niche audiences—"true believers" who are not looking for objective reporting but for commentators to present versions of the news that will strike a chord with their own personal biases. Indeed, Fox News commentators readily admit that their audience is drawn from people who are frustrated with the mainstream media, which they have accused of harboring a liberal bias. "[Fox News viewers] are so starved for someone to treat them well, someone to feed them some meat, not just cookies all the time,"[17] said Glenn Beck, a former Fox News commentator. According to Diana Mutz, professor of political science and communications at the University of Pennsylvania, "It's nothing new for people to seek media with their values ... Cable now offers people more choices; it can narrowcast to smaller, yet still profitable audiences."[18]

NON-AMERICAN NEWS OUTLETS

"News outlets like CNN and ABC News might have the biggest audiences, but the most trusted news outlets in America are actually British, according to a 2014 study from Pew Research Center."

—Pamela Engel, politics editor for *Business Insider*

Pamela Engel, "These Are the Most and Least Trusted News Outlets in America," *Business Insider*, March 27, 2017. www.businessinsider.com/most-and-least-trusted-news-outlets-in-america-2017-3.

Entertaining and Misleading

As cable commentators withhold facts or embellish the truth, their viewers sit at home absorbing those messages. Studies have started to show that many viewers have been unable to cut through the noise of what they hear and see on TV and the Internet and have developed some serious misperceptions about world events. For example, a study by the University of Maryland's Program on International Policy Attitudes concluded that viewers of Fox News harbor many common misperceptions about the Iraq War, including the idea that Iraq played a role in the 2001 terrorist attacks on the World Trade Center in New York and the Pentagon in Washington, D.C., or that deposed Iraqi dictator Saddam Hussein was developing weapons of mass destruction (WMDs). Such theories have been raised over the years by people who supported the Iraq War but were eventually disproven by military officials, diplomats, and intelligence experts. However, the Maryland study found that many Fox News viewers continued to believe they were true.

In a less scientific experiment, staffers of *Jimmy Kimmel Live!* went out onto the street in 2013 to ask people whether they preferred Obamacare or the Affordable Care Act (ACA). These are two names for the same health care program; however, many conservative news outlets dislike the ACA and call it Obamacare as a derogatory term. It has been called Obamacare so often that the name has stuck, and many people are unaware its true name is the ACA—something that was proven when people answered the staffers' question by saying that they were strongly against one program and believed the other was much better. The answers they gave depended on their political views: People who supported Obama tended to say Obamacare was better than the ACA, and the reverse was true for people who disliked Obama.

Throughout the 2016 presidential election process, the ACA was a major part of both candidates' platforms, so it was featured in the news often. Some news outlets called it Obamacare while others called it the ACA, and reporters sometimes made it clear that these were the same program, but sometimes they did not. In 2017, *Jimmy Kimmel Live!* repeated the experiment to see if the heavy news coverage of the issue had made people aware that the programs were one and the same. However, they found many people who still believed they were different. *Jimmy Kimmel Live!* is an entertainment program, not a news program, so it only aired interviews with people who were unaware of the difference, as this is generally funnier to audiences; most likely, there were many people who knew the correct answer to the question. In addition, the interviewers asked questions in a slightly tricky way. For instance, at one point, an interviewer asked, "What is the main difference between Obamacare and the Affordable Care Act?" Obviously the correct answer would be that there is no difference, but the interviewee hesitantly responded, "One is you pay, and the other one is Obama pays ... for you."[19] This shows that not only does the media often not give all the facts about an issue, but also that people tend to have difficulty sorting out the information they hear from different sources.

Partially because former Iraqi dictator Saddam Hussein—whose statue is shown here being toppled by Iraqi citizens—was already widely disliked, even by his own people, many Americans continued to believe he was developing WMDs.

Additionally, when people hear different statements from different sources, they tend to assume that one of those facts is actually a lie—and often they pick the statement they most agree with as the truth rather than the one that has the most evidence to back it up. This was demonstrated in the University of Maryland study when the study's authors found that consumers of non-cable media have misperceptions about the war as well as other issues, but in each case, the misperceptions held by Fox News viewers were wider and more forceful than those held by others. For example, the study found that one-third of Fox News viewers continued to believe Iraq developed WMDs even after a thorough investigation by the military found no such evidence. Meanwhile, 23 percent of CBS News viewers believed that idea, while 17 percent of print media readers and 11 percent of PBS viewers and National Public Radio (NPR) listeners continued to believe that Iraq maintained a weapons program. The authors of the Maryland study suggested that CBS, NPR, and newspapers have generally reported the news of the war more accurately than cable news networks, and therefore, people who consume news from those sources but still believe Iraq developed WMDs may simply have not been paying close attention when the truth about Iraq's weapons program was revealed. As for the viewers of Fox News, the study found they tend to pay particularly close attention to the Fox broadcasts. The authors of the study wrote,

> It would seem natural to assume that misperceptions are due to a failure to pay attention to the news and that those who have greater exposure to the news would have fewer misperceptions. This was indeed the case with those primarily [getting] their news from print media. However, for most media outlets, increased attention did not reduce the likelihood of misperceptions. Most striking, in the case of those who primarily watched Fox News, greater attention to news modestly increases the likelihood of misperceptions.[20]

The implications of the University of Maryland study are clear: Many cable news viewers pay close attention to what they see and hear, and what they see and hear quite often falls short of the truth. Frequently, when they do eventually hear the truth, they will assume it was made up to promote a particular agenda and dismiss it as "fake news" rather than doing their own research and getting all the facts.

GIVING THE PEOPLE WHAT THEY WANT

"Why would so many people be watching us if they didn't think we were doing something right?"

—Shepard Smith, Fox News anchor

Quoted in John Timpane, "In the Obama age, Fox News Finds the Right Stuff," Pop Matters, May 6, 2009. www.popmatters.com/article/92754-in-the-obama-age-fox-news-finds-the-right-stuff/

Opinionated, Dramatic, and Biased

As people have shown an increasing preference for biased news, it is unsurprising that extremely biased entertainment shows have grown incredibly. *The Daily Show* with Jon Stewart pioneered this trend. Stewart became the host of *The Daily Show* in 1999 and, over the course of his 16-year run, helped turn it into one of the most popular shows on TV. He mainly targeted politicians but also found that he could get a lot of laughs by making fun of cable TV journalists. Each night, Stewart would run clips of cable news reporters overdramatizing the news, showing their obvious biases and fumbling with the high-tech graphics that often dominate the TV screens as much as the news they are meant to illustrate. In 2015, Stewart stepped down as host, and Trevor Noah kept the show going.

Media critic Steve Young suggested that Stewart earned the trust of viewers because—unlike many cable news commentators—he did not try to represent opinions and drama as news, but told his viewers right up front that what they were about to see was all in fun. Young said, "While Stewart spins the news for laughs, O'Reilly spins it for partiality."[21] In other words, while Stewart was attempting to expose bias, O'Reilly was attempting to influence viewers' opinions. However, it is true that Stewart had his own, frequently liberal biases and sometimes used his show to condemn the actions of some politicians, giving his own opinion of the news pieces he featured. As *The Daily Show* exploded in popularity, other shows followed, most notably *The Colbert Report*—in which host Stephen Colbert played a conservative character pretending to be outraged at the liberal media—and *Last Week Tonight with John Oliver*.

As many cable news producers have learned, providing Americans with a fair and balanced interpretation of the news is proving difficult and is not always welcomed by cable viewers. In fact, up until January 2017, Fox News's motto was "Fair and Balanced," but that was replaced with "Most Watched, Most Trusted"—although Fox News executives stated the decision had nothing to do with its programming and was simply a marketing strategy. Clearly, judging by the ratings racked up by MSNBC and Fox News, Americans prefer their cable news served with strong doses of opinion, drama, theatrics, and bias. Other news shows have taken this strategy and run with it. For instance, on *The Alex Jones Show*, Alex Jones frequently presents conspiracy theories as if they are fact, getting extremely angry and ranting about them at length. John Oliver called him "a charismatic performer who gets charged up on a regular basis."[22] In one widely seen example, Jones reported that the armed forces were putting chemicals into water in an attempt to turn enemies of the United States gay. Jones yelled while hitting his desk, "What do you think tap water is? It's a gay bomb, baby … You think I am … shocked by it so I'm up here bashing it because I don't like gay people? I don't like them putting chemicals in the water that turn the … frogs gay! Do you understand that?"[23] Jones's anger often strikes a chord with viewers, despite the fact that he gets angry over things that are frequently proven to be untrue. His website, Infowars, is well known for publishing fake news stories.

Although The Daily Show *was meant to be satirical, it still maintained a level of journalistic integrity by keeping its viewers informed of the current issues.*

Fake News: The Return of Yellow Journalism

In the 19th century, rival New York City newspaper publishers Joseph Pulitzer and William Randolph Hearst were in a fierce competition for newspaper sales. Pulitzer's *New York World* printed a popular cartoon drawn by Richard F. Outcault called *Hogan's Alley* featuring a character called the Yellow Kid. Recognizing the value of the cartoon, Hearst hired Outcault to work for his *New York Journal*. The resulting profit-driven conflict for the Yellow Kid led to the term yellow journalism.

Yellow journalism refers to the sensationalist reporting of world events as a means of increasing profits. At this time, the island of Cuba was a colony in the Spanish Empire. Cuba had been home to a growing revolutionary movement for several decades, and the United States was pressuring the Spanish to withdraw from the island. Pulitzer and Hearst focused a great deal of attention on the conflict, publishing dramatic headlines, exaggerated stories of Spanish cruelty, and tales of the heroic revolutionaries. Accuracy and impartiality were forgotten in the pursuit of sales and profit.

In an attempt to resolve tensions between the United States and Spain, the U.S. Navy sent a battleship, the *Maine*, to Havana harbor. However, on February 15, 1898, an explosion sank and destroyed the *Maine*. While witnesses and a report by the Cuban government agreed the explosion occurred on the ship, Hearst instead spread rumors of a plot to sink the ship. The misreporting of events capitalized on anti-Spanish feelings shared by politicians and the public alike. When a U.S. investigation declared the *Maine* was destroyed by a mine in the harbor, the yellow journalists called for war. Within a few months, the United States carried the sentiment to a breaking point and declared war.

While these events actually occurred and anti-Spanish feelings had existed for some time, the public perception and reaction to them was most significant. By reporting in this polarizing manner, the press was able to manipulate the public perception of international events. Instead of a peaceful resolution to an unfortunate incident, escalating outrage led to war.

Newspapers' sensationalist reporting played a part in the Spanish-American War in 1898. Today, yellow journalism has the same dangerous potential.

So-called fake news has only become more polarizing and confusing over the years. As social media has become a common source of news and current events, Americans are encountering more inaccurate or unverified news stories everyday. In the wake of the 2016 presidential election, the Pew Research Center found that 64 percent of Americans believed fake news stories have been causing a great deal of confusion and misinformation about current events and the facts surrounding them. Only 11 percent of respondents felt fake news did not cause significant confusion. Although it is difficult to determine how much fake news people are seeing, the perception that these stories are damaging is widely agreed upon.

Americans also agree that action must be taken to prevent the spread of misleading fake news stories. Many respondents wanted the government and elected officials to prevent the spread of misinformation. They also wanted social media websites and Internet search engines to take action against fake news stories. In addition, most agreed that the public was also responsible for preventing made-up stories from being spread. While more than 80 percent of individuals surveyed believed they were able to identify fake news stories, nearly 23 percent admitted that they had knowingly or unknowingly shared a story which was fake.

Satire or Fake News?

Satire is a type of writing that uses exaggeration and sarcasm to make a point in a humorous way, but many people have difficulty telling the difference between fake news and satire. Sometimes this is because the satirical articles are not written well. If they are too close to the truth or sound too much like something a reasonable person might say, the humor will not come through. Some websites that publish satirical articles do this on purpose to confuse people. Other times, people cannot tell the difference because they are unfamiliar with satire.

One way to tell the difference between the two is to check which website an article is coming from. Some well-known satirical websites are *The Onion*, Clickhole, Reductress, and Above Average. These websites do not post anything truthful, but sometimes people are fooled into thinking what they are reading is serious. For instance, *The Onion* posted an article in 2004 titled "Study: 58 Percent of U.S. Exercise Televised." According to the *Huffington Post*,

> *Deborah Norville stated on her MSNBC show that a new study said that 58 percent of exercise done in America was on broadcast television. Whoever wrote the script that night literally wrote, "For instance, of the 3.5 billion sit-ups done during 2003, [2,030,000] of them were on exercise shows on Lifetime or one of the ESPN channels," [a clearly sarcastic joke from the article] as if it were news copy.*[1]

1. "17 Times 'The Onion' Fooled People Who Should Know Better," *Huffington Post*, September 25, 2012. www.huffingtonpost.com/2012/09/25/fooled-by-the-onion_n_1912413.html.

Opposition to Fake News

Social media websites have started taking action to stop the spread of fake news and to educate their users on how to identify false information. Following the 2016 U.S. presidential election, Facebook released the following guidelines:

1. **Be skeptical of headlines.** *False news stories often have catchy headlines in all caps with exclamation points. If shocking claims in the headline sound unbelievable, they probably are.*

2. **Look closely at the URL.** *A phony or look-alike URL may be a warning sign of false news. Many false news sites mimic authentic news sources by making small changes to the URL. You can go to the site to compare the URL to established sources.*

3. **Investigate the source.** *Ensure that the story is written by a source that you trust with a reputation for accuracy. If the story comes from an unfamiliar organization, check their "About" section to learn more.*

4. **Watch for unusual formatting.** *Many false news sites have misspellings or awkward layouts. Read carefully if you see these signs.*

5. **Consider the photos.** *False news stories often contain manipulated images or videos. Sometimes the photo may be authentic, but taken out of context. You can search for the photo or image to verify where it came from.*

6. **Inspect the dates.** *False news stories may contain timelines that make no sense, or event dates that have been altered.*

7. **Check the evidence.** *Check the author's sources to confirm that they are accurate. Lack of evidence or reliance on unnamed experts may indicate a false news story.*

8. **Look at other reports.** *If no other news source is report-ing the same story, it may indicate that the story is false. If the story is reported by multiple sources you trust, it's more likely to be true.*

9. **Is the story a joke?** *Sometimes false news stories can be hard to distinguish from humor or satire. Check whether the source is known for parody, and whether the story's details and tone suggest it may be just for fun.*

10. **Some stories are intentionally false.** *Think critically about the stories you read, and only share news that you know to be credible.*[24]

There is no way to completely prevent the spread of fake stories on social media, but individuals can avoid being part of the problem by not sharing unverified stories. It is important to always check whether information is trustworthy or deliberately misleading.

These guidelines help inform readers of how to spot the fake news stories and empower them to think critically about the information they are being presented with. Additionally, CBS News released a list of 22 fake news websites that are designed to look like real news outlets, including Infowars, 70News, *World News Report*, the *Boston Tribune*, the *Christian Times*, and more. Some are deliberately spreading false information, others are doing so by accident, and still others are intended to be satire. One website, called Newslo, has both factual and satirical stories on its website, which makes it difficult at times for readers to tell what is true and what is not.

The Internet and Journalism

In the last two decades, the Internet has become such an important part of most societies that many people feel they would not be able to get along without it. The Internet has become most people's source for information. However, since the Internet is relatively new, society is still trying to figure out the best way to navigate it. There are few laws regulating what someone can post online, and there are so many websites that it is impossible for someone to regulate or report on all of them. Therefore, someone who stumbles across a little-known website claiming to tell the truth about issues the mainstream media will not report may never see anything negative written about that particular website, which can lead them to believe that what they are reading is true. In reality, Internet news suffers from many of the same issues as mainstream news. Sometimes it is accurate, but at other times, authors betray their own biases. People must be just as critical about things they see on blogs as they are about things they read in a major newspaper or see on a cable news show.

Bloggers, some of whom consider themselves citizen journalists, have become more influential as Internet access has greatly expanded in recent years.

PROFESSIONALS AND AMATEURS

"Citizen journalists simply don't have the resources to bring us reliable news. They lack not only expertise and training, but connections and access to information."

–Andrew Keen, author of *The Cult of the Amateur: How Today's Internet Is Killing Our Culture*

Andrew Keen, *The Cult of the Amateur: How Today's Internet Is Killing Our Culture.* New York, NY: Doubleday, 2007, pp. 48–49.

The Internet is sometimes referred to as "the new media," and with good reason. Considering that daily newspapers date back more than 300 years (*The Daily Courant*, first published in London in 1702, is regarded as the first English-language daily newspaper), web-based media is, at this point, still in its infancy, but it has grown quickly. Today there are hundreds of millions of websites, instant messaging systems, social networking platforms, online stores, online auctions, classified ads, and blogs. The first blogs appeared in the early 1990s, and it was not long before people began airing their political opinions online.

Smartphones and tablets can be used to record and share an event with the world almost instantly. However, amateur journalists may not have the ethics or skills to report events without bias or misinformation.

Political Blogs

As blogs started dominating the Internet, liberal and conservative activists realized the potential of the medium to spread their messages. Soon they established their own websites to report both the news and their opinion of it. According to Mary-Rose Papandrea, a University of North Carolina law professor who published a 2007 study on political blogs, "One main reason blogs have proliferated [increased] is the absence of barriers to entry: a website can be created in minutes at little or no cost. Blogs cover every sort of imaginable issue. Although many of these millions of blogs are simply online diaries, political blogs are some of the most popular and well-known contributors to the public debate."[25]

On the left, among the most popular websites are the *Huffington Post* and *Daily Kos*. The *Huffington Post* was established by Arianna Huffington, a wealthy Californian who was at one time a conservative activist but changed her politics in the late 1990s, embracing liberal causes. One section of the website features guest posts from bloggers, most of whom are liberal. The *Huffington Post* can generally be relied upon to report facts correctly, but stories often have a liberal slant to them.

Daily Kos was established in 2004 by Markos Moulitsas Zúniga, a Californian whose family fled the civil war in El Salvador in the 1980s. When he joined the U.S. Army in 1989, he was a Republican, but he became a Democrat shortly after enlisting in the military. Following his service, he obtained his law degree and moved to San Francisco, California, a city that has always had a lot of liberal activism. Moulitsas's website features dozens of bloggers a day and reaches several million readers a month. *Daily Kos* has an even more obvious liberal slant than the *Huffington Post* and may sometimes report stories in a way that makes conservative politicians and policies look worse than they are. Other left-leaning websites tend to be more opinionated, including *Mother Jones* and *The Young Turks*.

On the right, a familiar complaint has prompted readers to seek out conservative bloggers: The mainstream media is too liberal and does not reflect their ideas and values, so they have chosen to go elsewhere for their news. According to conservative blogger John Hinderaker,

It's easier for conservatives to be heard now than it was 10 or 15 years ago primarily because of the new media. Virtually every newspaper in the United States … [is] all run by liberals. The news magazines are all liberal in orientation. The television networks are all liberal. And so I think that on talk radio, initially, and then followed up on the Internet, there's a lot more balance.[26]

One of the most popular conservative bloggers is Michelle Malkin. She oversees two blogs—*Michelle Malkin* and *Hot Air*—and she often posts guest articles on other blogs. In 2008, a website called Conservatism Today ranked *Hot Air* as the top conservative blog site on the Internet. "A conservative could get all his news from Hot Air and not miss anything of major significance," the review stated. "At any given time, nearly everything that has happened in politics that is of note to conservatives can be found on the front page."[27]

Other conservative blogs include *Townhall, Breitbart News,* and the *Daily Caller.* As more and more reputable news sources feature their own blog sections, including the *New York Times* and the *Washington Post,* it is getting increasingly difficult for readers to tell what is a legitimate news source and what is opinion-based, biased reporting. This is especially true when people title their blogs in a way that mimics longstanding newspapers—for example, putting words such as "news," "post," "gazette," and "times" in their name. Unfortunately, there is not yet an easy solution to this problem; currently, it is up to the reader to investigate multiple news sources in order to form their own opinion instead of automatically believing everything they read.

EVERYBODY CHOOSES

"Average people get to shape the outcome, like *American Idol.* This is not a couch-potato age. Average people are expecting to be part of the process."

—Simon Rosenberg, Democratic Party strategist, on using the Internet to connect with voters

Quoted in Philip Elliott, "Obama Turns to Web to Take Questions from Public," *Charlottesville Daily Progress,* March 26, 2009. www.dailyprogress.com/cdp/news/national/national_govtpolitics/article/obama_turns_to_web_to_bypass_news_media/37757.

According to the BBC, some fake news websites are motivated by fun and profit. Allen Montgomery, the founder of a website called The National Report, which intentionally publishes fake stories, said, "There are highs that you get from watching traffic spikes and kind of baiting people into the story. I just find it to be a lot of fun."[28] The BBC added that "there is big money to be made from sites [such as] The National Report which host web advertising, and these potentially huge rewards entice website owners to move away from funny satirical jokes and towards more believable content because it is likely to be more widely shared."[29] When people are outraged by something, they tend to

Obama Online

The Internet has provided political leaders with a way to communicate with voters without relying on the mainstream media. Shortly after he took office in 2009, President Barack Obama held a town hall meeting in the White House, taking questions from an audience of about 100 people as well as several questions submitted by people over the Internet.

More than 100,000 questions were submitted to the president over the Internet. He could answer only a small fraction of the questions, but he found the forum to be an effective way of getting his message directly to the voters, free of interpretation or bias that may be included in reports filed by journalists.

"In the new world of online media, formal press conferences are just one element or program to get the message out—to those, usually older, who watch such things on TV," said Morley Winograd, senior fellow at the University of Southern California's Annenberg Center on Communication Leadership and Policy, which studies the influence of the Internet on society. "The online version [Obama] is doing is an alternative way to get out the same message ... targeted toward a different audience, usually younger."[1]

1. Quoted in Philip Elliott, "Obama Turns to Web to Take Questions from Public," *Charlottesville Daily Progress*, March 26, 2009. 1. www.dailyprogress.com/cdp/news/national/national_govtpolitics/article/obama_turns_to_web_to_bypass_news_media/37757.

share it on social media. According to Montgomery, some of the stories on The National Report have earned as much as $10,000 because of how much they were shared.

No Story Too Small

By the early years of the 21st century, it was estimated that about 500,000 active blogs were on the Internet, including many devoted to politics and other issues found in the news. Bloggers soon proved themselves resourceful journalists, finding stories ignored by the mainstream media. For example, mostly through the efforts of bloggers, one of the most powerful political leaders in Washington, D.C., took a tumble.

In 2002, Senator Trent Lott of Mississippi spoke at Senator Strom Thurmond's 100th birthday party. Thurmond, of South Carolina, planned to retire a few weeks later after serving nearly 50 years in the Senate. Back in the 1940s, before joining the Senate, Thurmond ran for president as the candidate of the States' Rights Democratic Party, which preached segregation and a continuation of the Jim Crow laws that for decades had denied rights to African Americans. When Lott spoke at Thurmond's birthday party, Lott was the Senate majority leader and therefore one of the most influential politicians in the nation's capital. At the party Lott said, "I want to say this about my state. When Strom Thurmond ran for president, we voted for him. We're proud of him. And if the rest of the country had followed our lead, we wouldn't have had all these problems over all these years, either."[30]

Lott most likely meant his remarks as nothing more than kind words for an aging colleague about to retire from public life. However, many people saw this as one of the Senate's most powerful leaders endorsing a horrific resumption of the nation's racist past. As it turned out, Lott's comments were not reported first in the mainstream media; instead, they turned up on the blog Talking Points Memo. Once Lott's comments were widely circulated on the Internet, the mainstream press caught up with the issue. Newspapers published stories, network TV newscasts aired features on the incident, and cable TV commentators discussed the consequences of Lott's poor choice of words. A story that had been broken by citizen journalists and circulated entirely on the Internet had finally made national headlines. "Pretty soon this story gathered momentum enough in the blogosphere to shake the foundations of traditional journalism," said journalist Joan Connell in an interview with PBS, "and then the traditional news organizations jumped on board. But this was something that was very grass-roots."[31] Lott's career quickly took a nosedive. He was forced to give up his post as majority leader and in 2007, resigned from the Senate.

Strom Thurmond (shown here) was a member of a political party whose platform included denying rights to African Americans. While this fact was forgotten or ignored by regular news media, bloggers were quick to remind the public of his unsavory past.

A similar event happened in 2016 regarding the Dakota Access Pipeline (DAPL), an oil pipeline that was proposed to run through the Standing Rock Indian Reservation. Many Native Americans who live on the reservation protested the DAPL because if the pipeline ever broke, it would pollute their drinking water. The DAPL affected a relatively small group of people, so most news networks never mentioned the protest at first. It became a national movement after people shared pictures and videos of the protest on Facebook and blogs. After finding out about it, many people donated money, food, and other materials to help keep the protest going. With more people paying attention, major news networks began covering it, but people still relied on live videos posted to Facebook to show them what was really happening at the camp, including some unethical police tactics, as these were generally left out of the mainstream news coverage.

The stories involving Trent Lott and Standing Rock showed blogging at its best. Those stories and others added a considerable degree of credibility to blogs, particularly blogs devoted to covering politics.

Blogs: Quality Not Guaranteed

While blogging can enable citizen journalists to use the powers of the Internet to uncover news and reveal truths, blogging is at its worst when bloggers act irresponsibly—spreading rumors, innuendo, misinformation, and biases on the Internet. Since there is no editor looking over their shoulders to make sure that what they publish on their website is fair, balanced, and accurate, bloggers generally have free rein to show their worst sides.

Some blogs are little more than long, rambling rants by anonymous bloggers whose entries contain numerous typographical errors as well as misspellings and misuses of grammar and punctuation—and if they cannot get the spelling or punctuation right, chances are the bloggers are not getting their facts straight, either. However, this does not mean that a blog with perfect spelling and grammar will be completely accurate. Poor

With the ease of posting information on the Internet, there are now many blogs spreading false or misleading information, such as the idea that the earth is flat. This belief has attracted a large following, despite scientific evidence proving otherwise.

writing is simply one hint that an article does not come from a reputable source.

Health scares are a good example of how blogging can quickly get out of control. Many people report rumors on their blogs that are spread through social media such as Facebook and Twitter, as well as other blogs, which makes the effect much worse. The news spreads so fast that people read the same rumor multiple times on multiple websites, not realizing that all these websites are taking their news from each other. One example was the Ebola scare in the United States in 2014. Ebola is a deadly disease, but it is very hard to catch. It cannot be spread through the air; someone must come into direct contact with the bodily fluid of an infected person who is showing symptoms. However, when a few people in the United States were found to have Ebola, many news outlets such as Fox News and MSNBC reported this as if the disease were going to spread like wildfire and kill everyone in the country, and bloggers added fuel to the fire. *Forbes* magazine reported some of the wildest online rumors:

> *Did you read the one about the Ebola victims who have risen from the dead to become zombies? Or the reported cases of the disease in California, Kansas City and the Bahamas? ...*

> *Take a little wander through the more obscure corners of the internet, and you'll discover that Ebola is airborne, it can only be destroyed by nuclear warheads, and the US government is planning to build death camps to intern the millions of victims who are inevitably going to come down with the disease. Either that, of course, or it's a bio-warfare weapon created by the US with Africa being used as a test laboratory ...*

> *More dangerously, drinking salt water has been claimed online to cure the disease, killing two people in Nigeria and hospitalizing dozens more.*[32]

Anything Goes

Another potential way in which blogging can turn irresponsible may be found in the interactive nature of the medium. On the one hand, bloggers can provide readers with the ability to have their voices heard that is often unavailable to them in the mainstream media. Indeed, for a reader to have their voice reported in a daily newspaper, it would require the reader to write a letter to the editor and the letter to be selected for publication and edited—a process that could take several days or weeks, if in fact the letter is selected for publication. Adding comments to a blog, however, can be accomplished in seconds, and while comments may be deleted if they are offensive, the ones that are published are often unedited. Publication is almost always guaranteed—even if what the contributor says is inaccurate, unfair,

Breaking News on Twitter

Over the years, Twitter has become an increasingly popular source of information on news and current events. Many official institutions maintain a Twitter account, and various news organizations and reporters frequently post stories on Twitter. Anyone can view or share a post, and information can spread quickly this way.

In January 2009, US Airways flight 1549 was forced to make an emergency landing in New York's Hudson River shortly after takeoff. Minutes after the crash, news and photos of the downed plane were spreading rapidly across Twitter and other blogging services. The event was documented and reported in real time by witnesses on their phones. The story broke on Twitter 15 minutes before mainstream media sources began reporting.

As the story spread, more and more information became available online in the form of blog posts, commentary, and videos of the ongoing rescue. This new form of reporting allowed anyone to learn about the event as it developed in real time. Much of the information on the incident has been shared and preserved on social media.

Twitter and other social media websites have been instrumental tools for reporting world events as they occur, such as the landing of US Airways flight 1549 (shown here).

and irresponsible. In some cases, comments are also edited by bloggers to present exactly what they want readers to see.

Elizabeth Osder, principal of an Internet business strategy group called the Osder Group, said blogs consist of "opinion without expertise, without resources, without reporting."[33] While this may not be true of all blogs, it is true of many of them.

As the readership statistics for some of the top blogs indicate, many people seem to prefer their news with a little bias. Rather than finding accurate and unbiased reporting, they find bloggers who speak to their passions and prejudices. Additionally, the interactive nature of blogs attracts many readers. According to Mitchell Stephens, a professor of journalism at New York University, "The efforts of mainstream American journalism to explore the territory beyond plain reporting of news have … been tentative, spotty and unreliable. So bloggers have stepped into the gap. Indeed, that is surely among the explanations for the rapid success of bloggers—opinionated, snarky, smart … They are not restricted by 'walls' between news and opinion."[34]

WHO CONTROLS THE MEDIA?

"It's easy to overstate the extent to which the new media have brought conservative voices a parity in the news media generally. I don't think it's happened. In some ways, liberal control over the media is stronger today than it's ever been."

–John Hinderaker, conservative blogger

Quoted in "The Conservative Critique and Rise of Conservative Media," PBS *Frontline: News War*, February 13, 2007. www.pbs.org/wgbh/pages/frontline/newswar/tags/conservative.html#4

Students seeking to gather research for school projects may encounter the same biases and limited backgrounds on the Internet as consumers of news. Without the very important history of what is behind the news, it may be difficult for students to detect bias in what they are reading, making it harder for them to find the answers they need. A book that explores all sides of a complicated issue may be a much more appropriate method of researching a topic than trying to pull together a string of facts from a variety of biased or misleading websites.

A 2016 study by Stanford University found that about 82 percent of students have difficulty telling the difference between legitimate news stories, ads that are sponsored by companies to promote a certain point, and news articles that are intentionally misleading. In one example, an article about toxic waste near a Japanese nuclear plant was accompanied by a picture of deformed flowers. Although there was no citation for the picture, many students who viewed the article believed, based on the headline, that the picture provided proof of the article's claims.

Some experts have offered tips to help young adults become more media literate. According to the *Wall Street Journal*,

> Rather than trusting the "about" section of a website to learn about it, teach them "lateral reading"—leaving the website almost immediately after landing on it and [researching] the organization or author. Also, explain to teens that a top ranking on Google doesn't mean an article is trustworthy. The rankings are based on several factors, including popularity.
>
> Students should learn to evaluate sources' reliability based on whether they're named, independent and well-informed or authoritative, says Jonathan Anzalone, assistant director of the Center for News Literacy at Stony Brook University in New York. Posts should cite multiple sources, and the information should be verifiable elsewhere, he says.[35]

Many young adults are also unaware that sponsored content is generally a less trustworthy source of information. In 2014, John Oliver reported on the problem of advertising and the news. Many news outlets rely on advertising to help them make enough money to do things such as pay their staff and pay for web hosting. However, this can sometimes create media bias. For instance, online newspapers are increasingly using a tactic called native advertising to attract companies. This involves disguising an ad as a legitimate news article so more people will click on it. The ads generally have small disclaimers at the top or bottom such as "sponsored content," then make a point that helps sell the advertiser's service or product.

Some people see no problem with native advertising because of the disclaimers. However, as Oliver pointed out:

> *But it is a problem though, because the consumer cannot tell the difference. A recent study showed that less than half of visitors to a news site could distinguish between native advertising and actual news. And of course they can't! Because it's supposed to blend in.*[36]

In addition to causing confusion among readers, native advertising can create media bias by compromising a news outlet's content. As an example, Oliver discussed an article published in *The Atlantic* that was sponsored by the Church of Scientology and was highly complimentary of the group and its leader. For people who were aware this was an advertisement, this made it difficult for them to trust the content of the ad and *The Atlantic*'s other articles. However, for those who were fooled into thinking it was true journalism, it may have had a different negative effect. Reading such a positive article in a news source that is generally considered trustworthy may have made people believe only positive things about the Church of Scientology. If they read anything negative in a later article, even if it is published in a different trustworthy news source, they may discount the facts in the second article because they go against the beliefs the person has already formed. This is why it is important for everyone—teens as well as adults—to be critical of what they read and examine both the source and any potential sponsors.

Other Sources of Bias

Political bias is most frequently mentioned in the discussion about media bias, but there are other forms of bias that also have an impact on the way a news story is reported, although these are frequently tied to political beliefs. For example, bias against black people may cause a news outlet to report on the Black Lives Matter (BLM) movement using language that implies the group's concerns are not real issues, while another news outlet may report on the same story in a way that supports BLM's actions. These biases can shape the way an individual views specific groups.

Bias Against Women in Politics

Many people hold a conscious or unconscious bias against women, especially in politics. For years, women were seen as too emotional or not smart enough to hold public office. Although they have made advancements in this area and many women have been elected to various positions, no woman has become president of the United States yet, partially because of this bias. Since 1872, several women have run for the nation's highest office. A few have campaigned as fringe or minor party candidates, whereas some have made legitimate efforts to seek the nominations of the two major parties. Erika Falk, program director of the Israel Institute, examined many of those campaigns and concluded that female candidates for president are often the victims of gender bias in the media.

Falk examined the media coverage of eight presidential campaigns and found that male candidates were the subject of twice as many stories as female candidates and that the stories written about male candidates were generally longer. Moreover, she said, the stories about the male candidates focused far more often on their positions on policies, whereas the stories about women tended to focus more on their personalities, backgrounds, and families. According to Falk, the gender bias found in the media coverage of presidential campaigns has an impact that goes beyond that year's presidential race. By not treating women as equal competitors for the presidency, she said, the press plays a role in maintaining the male domination of politics. She said fewer women are encouraged to enter politics because they find fewer role models holding high political office.

NEWS FOR EVERYONE

"The media report and write from the standpoint of the white man's world ... This may be understandable, but it is not excusable in an institution that has the mission to inform and educate the whole of our society."

−1968 report of the National Advisory Commission on Civil Disorder

Quoted in Virginia Whitehouse, "Coverage of Racial Tension," *World & I*, February 2003, p. 62.

This gender bias was evident during Hillary Clinton's presidential campaigns. Despite the obstacles faced by women in politics, then-senator Hillary Clinton of New York managed to break into the top tier of candidates competing for the presidency in the 2008 election. Still, Clinton found herself fighting against gender bias in the media. According to Falk, when Clinton announced her candidacy, 36 major daily newspapers covered the event and published stories. At the time, Falk said, then-senator Barack Obama of Illinois was trailing well behind Clinton in the polls. However, when Obama announced his candidacy, 59 big-city daily newspapers covered the story. Falk said the bias shown in the Clinton-Obama race was simply another case of the press focusing more on male candidates. "The most striking finding was that women consistently got less coverage than male candidates in the same race, and that did not improve over time,"[37] Falk said.

Although she was highly qualified and experienced, gender bias in reporting continually undermined Hillary Clinton's presidential campaigns.

Other observers believe the bias against Clinton went beyond the news columns of daily newspapers—that Clinton was also treated unfairly by other media, particularly the cable TV commentators who often criticized her clothing and appearance. Her relationship with her husband, former president Bill Clinton, was also the subject of jokes. Bill had been unfaithful to Hillary during his presidency, and many people seemed to falsely believe this was a reflection of her presidential abilities. After Clinton won the New Hampshire primary in 2008, Bill

Kristol, editor of the conservative *Weekly Standard*, suggested that female voters cast their ballots for Clinton out of sympathy or support for a fellow woman rather than because they agreed with her positions on the war in Iraq, the economy, health care, and other important issues.

Such comments by male journalists reinforced the opinions many women have held about gender bias in the media—that even when a prominent woman steps forward and wins a hotly contested race, male journalists can be counted on to attribute the win to factors that have nothing to do with her ability to govern. "Sen. Hillary Clinton's run for the Democratic nomination has been fraught with sexism, exposing an ugly streak within the American press," media critic Jessica Wakeman wrote. "Degrading ... attacks on Clinton spanned from print to radio, from the Web to television."[38]

The situation did not improve when Clinton ran again in 2016. She was attacked by her opponent, Donald Trump, for not having a "presidential look"[39] and for not having enough stamina, or strength, to perform her presidential duties, which many interpreted to mean that he believed Clinton is weaker because she is a woman. When news outlets reported on the candidates, some showed a moderate gender bias. For instance, after one debate, Fox News host Brit Hume described the candidates differently:

> Hume ... described Trump as looking "annoyed" and "put out," but the host didn't stop there. He added that Clinton seemed "composed, smug sometimes," but "not necessarily attractive." Hume later clarified that he was "talking about demeanor." On social media, many were quick to point out that Hume said nothing about Trump's attractiveness, but was quick to critique Clinton's debate performance alongside her physical attractiveness.[40]

According to polls conducted after the election, only 38 percent of voters said Trump was qualified to be president. However, he still won the election, and many people believe the way the media reported on the candidates played a role in his victory.

Subtle Bias

Some examples of bias are obvious, but others are very subtle and easy to miss. One source of subtle bias is the words an author chooses. Accuracy in Media (AIM), a group that points out instances of liberal media bias, gave one example:

Which version sounds less biased to you?

A. *"Heart-wrenching tales of hardship faced by people whose care is dependent on Medicaid"*

B. *"Information on the lifestyles of Medicaid dependents" ...*

Everyone who uses words is guilty of using biased word choice—even those writers out there who consciously attempt to use neutral language. That's because everyone has a unique worldview, and that worldview tends to express itself whether obvious or not.[1]

Being aware of this type of bias can help readers and viewers spot it and decide whether or not they agree with a reporter's word choice and worldview.

Another example of subtle bias is the types of photos that are shown alongside a story. For instance, during the 2016 presidential election, news outlets that were left-leaning would generally show pictures that made Clinton look professional and Trump look angry, while right-leaning news outlets often showed Trump looking dignified and Clinton looking silly.

Word choice and photo choice are often combined to pack an extra powerful punch. For instance, in 2015, two groups of men were arrested for burglary, and both stories, written by the same journalist, were published in the Iowa newspaper *The Gazette*. The first group, three white men, were University of Iowa students who were on the wrestling team. They were described in terms of their accomplishments—"Three University of Iowa Wrestlers Arrested, Suspended"[2]—and their yearbook photos were published with the article. The second group consisted of four black men; the article mentioned that they had behaved violently, and instead of yearbook photos, their police mug shots were used. This difference made the group of white men look much more respectable than the group of black men. After the difference was pointed out on multiple other websites, *The Gazette* published the white men's mug shots as well as an explanation of its original photo choice.

The same thing has happened to victims of police violence; the police officer is generally shown smiling in uniform, while the victim—frequently a black man—is shown looking threatening. This has led to the viral hashtag #IfTheyGunnedMeDown, in which black people share two different photos of themselves side by side as a way to show that everyone, no matter their race, has different sides to their personality. The hashtag refers to black people questioning which photo the media would share if they were victimized: one in which they look respectable, or one in which they look silly or threatening?

1   Allie Duzett, "Media Bias in Strategic Word Choice," Accuracy in Media, April 28, 2011. www.aim.org/on-target-blog/media-bias-in-strategic-word-choice/

2   Lee Hermiston, "Three University of Iowa Wrestlers Arrested, Suspended," The Gazette, March 30, 2015. www.thegazette.com/subject/news/three-university-of-iowa-wrestlers-arrested-20150324

Discrimination Against the LGBT+ Community

The gender bias that surfaced during Clinton's campaigns was rarely subtle—the commentaries on Clinton's apperance and choice of clothing were hard to miss. Likewise, members of the LGBT+ community are often depicted poorly in the media.

For example, in January 2008 readers of the *New York Post* opened their newspapers to find this headline: "Evil Lesbian Mom Left Toddler to Die Slow Death: DA."[41] The story described a murder in which a 23-month-old boy had been abused by the girlfriend of the boy's mother, sustaining injuries that proved fatal. The woman who hurt the boy was convicted in the murder and sentenced to a prison term of 15 years to life.

Leaders of the LGBT+ community protested that the headline was written to make LGBT+ people seem naturally bad. "Such a gratuitous description would not have been used were the [defendants] straight,"[42] complained Neil G. Giuliano, president of the Gay and Lesbian Alliance Against Defamation (GLAAD). The headline implied that being a lesbian had something to do with the woman's violent act, when in fact this is untrue; many heterosexual people commit violent acts as well, and sexuality has nothing to do with a person's morals.

Homophobic and transphobic sentiments are still very common in mainstream media. Despite great strides in equal rights, the LGBT+ community and its allies constantly have to fight prejudice and hate.

To Giuliano and other gay rights activists, the headline in the *Post* story confirmed what they have known for years—that the media shows a bias against the LGBT+ community. Although the *New York Post* ignored GLAAD's demands that it change its tone when describing LGBT+ people, other media outlets have responded. In May 2009, *Esquire* magazine published a story that was intended to be funny, claiming to teach its largely male readership the proper ways in which to use profanity. In the story, though, the author used derogatory expressions for gay people. GLAAD responded quickly and issued a complaint with David Granger, *Esquire*'s editor at that time, who acknowledged that the magazine had done something wrong. In an apology published online and in the magazine's June issue, the magazine wrote, "The target of the parody was profanity itself and not the various people who might be its object, including gay people. But we used a particularly offensive phrase we shouldn't have. It certainly was not our intent to cause pain. Judging from the reaction, we did. For that we are sincerely sorry."[43]

Religious Bias

Both right-leaning and left-leaning news sources have been accused of religious bias in their reporting. People who identify as conservative are often Christian, while people who identify as liberal generally represent a wider range of religious views. For this reason, right-leaning news sources are more likely to report stories of anti-Christian bias, while left-leaning ones are more likely to report bias against other religions. For instance, around December, conservative news outlets—particularly Fox News—frequently report about the "war on Christmas," which is a perceived attack on the holiday. The channel airs stories about companies wishing its customers "Happy Holidays" instead of "Merry Christmas" and point out Christmas merchandise that has a winter theme, but nothing to do with Jesus. In the view of people who believe there is a war on Christmas, Christians are being persecuted and prevented from celebrating their holiday. Liberal news outlets often disagree with this view, stating that other religions are far more oppressed in Western society than Christians are and that no one is preventing

Christians themselves from saying "Merry Christmas" or using religious decorations.

On the other side of the spectrum, many liberal news outlets take issue with the media's reporting in regard to other religions, especially Islam. After a comment from a CNN anchor attacking the Muslim community in general, the *Huffington Post* wrote,

> *It's not just the fear-mongers at Fox News, who exploit terrorist attacks to fuel anti-Muslim hostility with such consistency it's almost not worth commenting on. It's the mainstream media, and while Islamophobia rears its head in print as well as online, it is most pronounced on television …*
>
> *"Journalists, especially TV journalists, love scoops," says Nathan Lean, a scholar at Georgetown University's Prince Alwaleed bin Talal Center for Muslim-Christian Understanding. "So what happens is a lot of them ask leading questions—they insinuate, infer, hypothesize: 'Could it have been an attack carried out by Al-Qaeda?' Then all of a sudden the conversation is dominated by Al-Qaeda."[44]*

This is one way media bias is responsible for the spread of misinformation. Many people may see the first few reports after an incident, in which the media questions whether certain groups are to blame, and take those as factual reports. Later, when the truth is reported, those same people may either not see the broadcast or assume the second report is the false one.

FIGHTING FOR YOUR RIGHTS

"The black press was the advocate of all our dreams, wishes, and desires. I still think it was [the] greatest advocate for equal and civil rights that black people ever had in America. It had an effect on everybody."

–Frank Bolden, former reporter for the black newspaper the *Pittsburgh Courier*

Quoted in *The Black Press: Soldiers Without Swords*, PBS, 1998. www.pbs.org/blackpress/film/fulltranscript.html.

Fighting Racial Bias

One way to get the media's attention is to form watchdog groups such as GLAAD, which can organize members of minority communities to stage boycotts and similar activities. Minority groups have also found another effective strategy for dealing with media bias: They simply go into the media business themselves.

By establishing their own newspapers and other media outlets, members of minority groups have been able to provide news coverage of the activities in their communities free of the biases they often find in the white-owned mainstream media. Indeed, the bias in the mainstream press was so deep that for many years big city newspapers and other important media outlets failed to report one of the major stories of the 20th century: the blossoming civil rights movement. It was not until the black press began reporting accurately and fairly the growing resentment among African Americans toward their status as second-class citizens that the mainstream media finally recognized the importance of the story.

In America, people of color have a long history of establishing newspapers, radio stations, and magazines, in many cases specifically because they did not believe their issues were covered fairly in the mainstream press. The first African American newspaper, *Freedom's Journal*, was established in New York City in 1827, founded specifically to counter the proslavery positions published in white-owned papers. From the 1890s through the early 1920s, while white-owned newspapers rarely reported the lynchings, or vigilante murders, of black people, the black-owned press published vivid accounts of the killings.

Sometimes the racial bias in the mainstream media was quite apparent to black readers. For example, white reporters made a point of identifying black people by their race. Black press historian James Grossman recalled, "One of the things that white newspapers did in the early 20th century was whenever they would mention somebody who was African American, they would put ... next to his or her name, (Negro). So it would say, 'Jack Johnson (Negro) won the world heavyweight championship yesterday.'"[45]

Taking Profit into Account

During his campaign for the presidency in 2008, Democrat Barack Obama made a trip to the war zones in Afghanistan and Iraq, followed by a speech in Berlin, Germany, before an estimated crowd of about 200,000 people. Three major American TV networks sent their anchors to cover the speech, while dozens of other reporters followed Obama as well. A few months earlier, Republican presidential candidate John McCain also toured the war zone in Iraq. None of the networks sent their anchors, and in comparison, the McCain visit received almost no coverage in the media.

Such an obvious difference raises the question of whether Obama received favorable treatment in the media, most likely because of his history-making campaign as the first major-party black candidate for president. In other words, some people believed reporters gave Obama favorable treatment because they did not want to be accused of racism.

Media critic John K. Wilson does not think that occurred. Wilson, who writes about the media for the advocacy group Fairness & Accuracy in Reporting, said Obama received preferential coverage because, as his speech in Berlin proved, he made more news. "Obama is on the cover of magazines because his face sells a lot more magazines than McCain's picture," Wilson wrote. "That's a pro-profit bias, not a liberal bias."[1]

During his first presidential campaign, Barack Obama's sensational rise in popularity led to a high level of media coverage.

1. John K. Wilson, "The Myth of Pro-Obama Media Bias," FAIR, September 15, 2008. fair.org/extra/the-myth-of-pro-obama-media-bias/.

Following World War II, the black press covered the growing civil rights movement in America, editorializing strongly for equality. During the 1950s, as the civil rights movement turned into a huge story, the mainstream media discovered that its news staffs were overwhelmingly white and that white reporters had few sources in the black community, so many of the best reporters from the black press were hired for jobs in big-city newsrooms, giving major newspapers as well as radio and TV broadcasters access to the important insiders in the civil rights movement. Frank Bolden, who had worked for the black newspaper the *Pittsburgh Courier*, found a job with the *New York Times*. Bolden said,

> *The black press made me conscious of the fact that I was truly an American and I deserved everything every other American got. If it did nothing more, it made me realize that separate does not mean equal. And ever since I worked at the Courier, I have been a battler and a champion for equal rights for all American citizens, regardless of their color, race, or creed. And now gender.*[46]

In 1975, 44 black journalists formed the organization that is known today as the National Association of Black Journalists. Many of its members work for the mainstream print and electronic media, but many more work for the black newspapers

The National Association of Black Journalists represents members of the black press and works against bias and discrimination in news media.

that continue to serve important functions in their communities. Such papers include the *Chicago Defender*, *Los Angeles Sentinel*, *Washington Afro-American*, *Philadelphia Tribune*, and *New York Amsterdam News*. More than 200 black newspapers are published in the United States, serving about 15 million readers. According to historian and author Charles A. Simmons, "The basic editorial philosophy of the black press has not changed much since 1827, when *Freedom's Journal* was founded. The goals of all editors were to deliver messages in unity to their readers, deliver them with passion and emotion, and let white editors and citizens know that black citizens were humans who were being treated unjustly."[47]

The Need for Diversity

Black journalists may have come a long way in recent years, but it would be naive to suggest that racial bias has disappeared from the media. John Leo, a media critic for *U.S. News & World Report*, suggested the media may treat issues of racial diversity so lightly because few American newsrooms reflect the true racial composition of American society. People of color make up one-third of the population of the United States, but most professional newsrooms fall far short of reflecting that diversity. In 2015, *The Atlantic* reported that the previous year, "all minority groups accounted for 22.4 percent of television journalists, 13 percent of radio journalists, and 13.34 percent of journalists at daily newspapers ... walk into most major newsrooms in the U.S. and you'll be overwhelmed by the whiteness and maleness of the editorial staff."[48] Some people believe this is because people of color are less likely to look for a career in journalism, but studies have shown this is untrue. People of color "made up 21.4 percent of graduates with degrees in journalism or communications between 2004 and 2014, but less than half of minority graduates found full-time jobs, while two-thirds of white graduates did."[49] This lack of diversity means the stories the mainstream media reports often do not take different points of view into account. Additionally, issues that affect primarily people of color, women, the LGBT+ community, and other groups are often not reported. Despite the best efforts of oppressed groups to be heard in the mainstream media, the bias they find in the press never seems to go away.

Is All Media Biased?

Although bias is part of human nature, some news reports are clearly more biased than others. Some news outlets are generally able to maintain a neutral tone. Some are also more willing to air contradictory information than others. New information is always coming to light, and something that is reported as fact one week may be disproven the following week. News outlets show bias when they are unwilling to report the conflicting information or if they report it as an instance of the other side's bias. For instance, Americans have been concerned about terrorism for years, and this fear increased dramatically after the attacks of September 11, 2001. For a long time, it was assumed that Americans were in immediate danger from terrorists, and many news outlets reported the government's ongoing efforts in what they called the "war on terror." However, recent studies have found that this fear has been blown out of proportion. The *Boston Globe* reported in February 2017 that more Americans are killed each year by carbon monoxide poisoning, falling furniture, and lightning strikes combined than by terrorists, and these statistics have been shown in multiple studies. However, some news outlets persist in reporting terrorism as if it is the most pressing danger Americans face.

In August 2017, *Adam Ruins Everything* aired a correction segment in which the host explained the ethics of correcting reporting mistakes and making new information known:

> We have gotten a few things wrong, but that doesn't ruin our show at all ... Our research team [spends] every day calling experts, combing through sources, and fact-checking scripts to ensure that the information we present on this show is as close to the truth as possible. But they're also human, and humans sometimes make mistakes ... It wouldn't be truthful to claim we were infallible. The intellectually honest thing to do is to be transparent about our process and public about our mistakes.[50]

All journalists will report something incorrect at one point or another, either because of human error or because new information comes to light later. Admitting mistakes is one important part of ethical journalism.

An Obligation to Objectivity

Many editors and reporters at mainstream news outlets—those who are on the front lines reporting and editing the news every day—take issue with critics who suggest that they permit their personal biases to interfere with their professional responsibilities to present the news to their readers. Most will admit to harboring personal biases—that is simply a part of being human—but they also insist that they do not permit their feelings about political or social issues to color their work as journalists.

One example is Fox News's Shepard Smith. Although Smith works at the conservative news channel and has conservative views, he generally seems to make an effort to report the news as truthfully as possible, even when it goes against the views of himself or the network. Fox News has often shown support for Donald Trump, while more liberal news outlets have tended to oppose him. However, in March 2017, Smith reported on a complex political event: the Trump administration's talks with the Russian government, which some people believed to be a betrayal of the U.S. government. Trump and his supporters insisted he had done nothing wrong, but several facts came to light showing that people in the Trump administration had lied regarding the situation. Some pro-Trump news outlets either did not report the lying or downplayed it so it seemed unimportant, but Smith tackled it head-on, saying to White House reporter Julie Bykowicz, "There's been a lot of lying, Julie ... There's been lying about who you talked to and ... almost inevitably and invariably, they were lying about talking to the Russians about something. It's too much lying and too much Russia and too much smoke and now they're investigating."[51] Smith went on to remind Bykowicz that Trump had called the Russia reports fake news while at the same time saying that the reports of secret dealings were real—both of which could not be true at the same time, as one statement contradicted the other. Some people applauded Smith while others believed it was inappropriate and inaccurate.

In another instance, after Hurricane Maria hit Puerto Rico in 2017, Smith debunked a false news story reported by his own network that supplies were not being distributed to Puerto Rican victims because truckers in Puerto Rico were on strike and refusing to deliver the items. Trump also blamed the truckers for not doing enough after Puerto Rican mayor Carmen Yulin Cruz criticized the Trump administration for the slow response of its aid. According to Smith,

> Of course, the president mentioned the truckers … The biggest problem on the island is the distribution of supplies, we're told … Some of the truckers can't be reached because there's no communication working in so many areas still.

> Reports that a union truckers' strike added to the problems are not true … They are, in fact, fake news, spread largely, it appears, by a website called Conservative Treehouse and then over Twitter and Facebook. Again, there is no trucker's strike. That's fake news. The truckers in Puerto Rico are victims too.[52]

PERSONAL PREJUDICES

"The perception of political bias stems from the reader's own prejudices that many readers refuse to admit they have."

–David Awbrey, former editorial page editor of the *Wichita Eagle*

David Awbrey, "Tugging at the Media's Curtain The Elite News-Gathering Organizations Are out of Touch with Common Americans and It Shows," *The Spokesman-Review*, June 23, 1996. www.spokesman.com/stories/1996/jun/23/tugging-at-the-medias-curtain-the-elite-news/.

Readers' Voices

News organizations are not insensitive to charges of bias. For example, many online newspapers have started publishing the contact information of the reporters who write the stories so readers can contact them directly to discuss issues of bias in their stories. Most also invite readers to add their own comments underneath the stories, which makes it easier for people to see others' support or objections.

Dave Winer, who runs the blog *Scripting News*, said his readers are constantly challenging his facts, which he feels has made him pay close attention to accuracy and fairness. "You're going to get fact-checked like no reporter has ever been fact-checked," he said. "You're going to have a thousand people read your blog, and they're all going to check your [facts] like you wouldn't believe."[53]

Winer said many bloggers have taken steps to help ensure fairness and guarantee accuracy to readers. According to Winer, many bloggers now include links to the source materials on which they base their commentaries. These sources often include news stories published on newspapers' websites, reports issued by government agencies, speeches by political leaders, and transcripts of testimony of witnesses who testify before congressional committees. Therefore, if a blogger takes issue with comments made by a politician, blog readers can instantly read what the politician had to say in their own words and judge for themselves. By making such sources available, Winer said, blog readers can immediately verify the accuracy and fairness of the bloggers' commentaries. Winer, a former writer for *Wired* magazine, said, "I know [American mainstream news outlets] have lots of inaccuracies. I know they get the story wrong a lot ... I don't think they get better quality than bloggers do; I think bloggers actually, if anything, get better quality."[54]

Dave Winer (shown here) has cautioned other bloggers that citations and links to more information are essential for maintaining accuracy and credibility online.

RESTORING FAITH IN THE MEDIA

"[A 2007 study] showed these media are doing the job they are supposed to do by providing fair and balanced coverage. It is important people hear this message because the misperception has a disenchanting effect."

—Philo Wasburn, Purdue University sociology professor

Quoted in Amy Patterson Neubert, "Prof: Misperception of Media Bias Causes Problems for Democracy," Purdue University, September 26, 2007. www.purdue.edu/uns/x/2007b/070926T-WasburnBias.html.

Staying Impartial

Mainstream news executives insist that objectivity is maintained on their nightly newscasts. At ABC, former anchor Charles Gibson, who retired in 2009, said he preserved his objectivity in reporting on politics by refusing to vote, denying himself a right of citizenship in order to maintain his objectivity. Moreover, he made it a point not to discuss personal politics with the ABC news staff. "I don't know the politics of anybody out there—we don't discuss it,"[55] Gibson said of the newsroom staff.

Early in 2008, NBC correspondent Lee Cowan admitted on the air that as he covered then-presidential candidate Barack Obama, he found himself overwhelmed by the thousands of people who were flocking to Obama's speeches. "From a reporter's point of view," Cowan admitted, "it's almost hard to remain objective. It's infectious, the energy, I think."[56] Critics immediately attacked Cowan and NBC for showing a bias toward Obama, but news anchor Brian Williams was quick to defend the network's objectivity. He said,

> Lee was talking about the swirl of excitement that has hit the Obama campaign ... the crowds, the hoopla—all of it. Today we learned that rival political efforts were spinning this as some kind of "bias" on the part of either Lee, or me, or this News Division, and that's just ridiculous. My response is as it always is in these situations: look at it again, listen to what's being said, and judge us by the quality and fairness of our journalism.[57]

Brian Williams (shown here) has asserted that there is a strong emphasis on objective reporting at NBC. However, some do not think his word is trustworthy after he was suspended for exaggerating a story.

Who Watches the Watchers?

Many groups are making it their business to judge the media for their accuracy and fairness. Some of these organizations have been funded by foundations and other nonpartisan, or nonpolitical, organizations to maintain a true public dialogue on press bias and similar issues that surround the news media. The intentions of other groups are not as clear. On the surface, these groups claim to monitor the media, but in some cases, they have hidden agendas: They have been established by liberal or conservative groups for the purpose of enhancing their arguments about bias.

One website, Media Bias/Fact Check, is a comprehensive list of news outlets grouped by bias. The categories of bias include left, left-center, least biased, right-center, right, pro-science, conspiracy-pseudoscience, questionable sources, and satire. Each entry includes where the news source falls on this spectrum, how trustworthy its facts are, and a short synopsis of the content and reliability of the source. For instance, in the case of the left-leaning feminist blog *Feministing*, Media Bias/Fact Check wrote,

> *In review, Feministing has a strong left wing bias in reporting as most articles favor the political left and criticize conservative policies. There is strong use of loaded words in headlines such as this: WHY JOE ARPAIO DESERVES TO BURN IN HELL (A LAUNDRY LIST). Interestingly, this same article is impeccably sourced to credible media sources and is 100% evidence based. So, while the headline may be sensational the content of the article is factual. Overall, we rate Feministing as left biased based on story selection and support of issues that are supported by the left. They are also factual in report-ing due to proper sourcing.*[58]

Another website dedicated to stopping the spread of false in-formation is Snopes. This website, which was founded in 1994 by David Mikkelson, employs dedicated fact-checkers who verify Internet rumors, viral social media posts, and questionable news re-ports. In one example, Snopes addressed a rumor that actress Ashley Judd "announced that she was moving to the Middle East, 'where women have more rights.'" Snopes fact-checker Dan Evon wrote,

> *In March 2017, actress Ashley Judd posted a link to a USA Today article concerning a proposed equal-rights amendment to the United States Constitution and how it relates to the issue of women's rights in countries around the world. She also included a partial quote from the article, which stated that the United States ranked 104th, behind countries such as Burundi, Serbia and Iraq …*
>
> *This tweet rankled some readers, who criticized Judd for saying that women in the Middle East had "more rights" than women in the United States. However, Judd never actually said that … Furthermore, two of the three countries mentioned in the USA Today quote—Burundi and Serbia—are not even Middle Eastern countries …*
>
> *The unreliable FreedomDaily.com was one of the first to claim that Judd said she wanted to move to the Middle East. Although the*

*headline blared, "Loud-Mouth Liberal Ashley Judd Wants To Live
In Middle East Where Women Have 'More Rights,' Gets Unexpect-
ed Surprise!," the idea for the actress to move [to] the Middle East
came from the author of this piece, not Judd: "Loud-mouth liberal
celebrity, Ashley Judd, sent Tweets saying America lacks behind
some other countries in equal rights for women. Does she want
to go live there then, because we can start a GoFundMe for her
one-way ticket to Burundi, Serbia, or Iraq, which apparently treat
women better than America …" Several other disreputable web
sites, with names like NewsBreaksHere, USANewsHouse, NewIn-
formation.Today, US Conservative, Daily News Cycle and To The
Death Media published similar stories, evidently just aggregating
[collecting] or recycling them from the first misleading claim without doing any further research.*[59]

When news outlets recirculate biased and untrue information,
people may read the same rumor dozens of times, making them
think it is the truth. Using websites such as Snopes and Media
Bias/Fact Check can help people avoid being tricked this way.

CYNICISM TOWARD THE MEDIA

"Credibility ratings for the major broadcast and cable outlets
have fallen in recent years, due in large part to increased
cynicism toward the media on the part of Republicans
and conservatives."

–Pew Research Center for U.S. Politics and Policy

"News Audiences Increasingly Politicized," Pew Research Center for U.S. Politics and Policy, June 8,
2004. www.people-press.org/2004/06/08/v-media-credibility-declines/.

Unfortunately, assessments produced by other so-called
media watchdog groups may not be as neutral as the groups
would like readers to believe. Many self-described media watchdog groups whose names would suggest impartiality actually
have hidden purposes. For example, Accuracy in Media (AIM)
and the Media Research Center are both sponsored by conservative activists and are dedicated to exposing what they believe to
be cases of liberal reporting.

AIM was financed largely by billionaire Richard Mellon Scaife, who was a political conservative and publisher of the conservative *Pittsburgh Tribune-Review*. A glance at the AIM website shows that it targets mostly liberal media outlets, accusing them of bias. The Media Research Center also searches for liberal bias in media coverage. Founded by conservative activist L. Brent Bozell III, the Media Research Center makes no secret of its distaste for the liberal media. At its headquarters in Reston, Virginia, the Media Research Center employs a team of analysts who spend their days watching cable broadcasts and picking through the print media, identifying bias where they see it. The center churns out a number of publications reporting on what it has identified as bias. Bozell also writes a column that is published in several conservative journals. The organization's website contains an extensive archive of what the Media Research Center believes to be examples of biased reporting by the liberal media.

In 2003, some media watchdogs protested the New York Times, *accusing it of publishing information that threatened national security.*

On the other side, the group Fairness & Accuracy in Reporting (FAIR) claims to be unbiased, but critics have complained that it more often finds fault with the conservative press than with the liberal press. FAIR was founded in 1986 by Jeff Cohen, whose background would certainly suggest a strong bias toward liberalism—he is a former staff attorney for the American Civil Liberties Union (ACLU) and a contributor to such politically liberal magazines as *Rolling Stone*, *Mother Jones*, and *New Times*. As with AIM and the Media Research Center, FAIR produces a number of publications and commentaries on media bias, often taking the approach that conservatives are favored in the media. FAIR also produces a weekly syndicated radio program, *CounterSpin*, in which commentators discuss media bias as they see it—often from the perspective that the media is biased in favor of conservatives.

With groups such as FAIR, AIM, and the Media Research Center closely monitoring the media, there is no shortage of evidence that would seem to show the media is very biased. An additional challenge for news consumers is to wade through the biases of the media watchdogs.

SHRUGGING OFF BIAS

"In the face of any and all personal feelings and emotions I harbored about our incursion in Iraq, I still had to fashion a daily [news] report about the war that was thorough, insightful and—above all—impartial in its presentation."

–Kent Cockson, former newspaper editor

Kent Cockson, "Shrugging Off Bias," American Society of News Editors, July 1, 2003. www.asne.org/index.cfm?ID=4756.

Finding a Balance

The credibility of the press and news media has seen a steady decline in recent years, and the question of believability and accuracy is regularly debated. A 2012 survey by the Pew Research Center showed how much the public trust in reporting has declined. The respondents were asked how believable they felt various news sources were. The survey showed that over the last decade, there has been a distinct decrease in credibility affecting national newspapers, cable news outlets, broadcast TV networks, and National Public Radio (NPR).

Open vs. Hidden Bias

Seth Ackerman, a contributor to *Extra!*, a magazine published by Fairness & Accuracy in Reporting (FAIR), believes bias in the media may not be such a bad thing. After all, he pointed out, British newspapers such as *The Times* of London, which is conservative, and the *Guardian*, which is liberal, have long been known for their biases. However, he says, each newspaper is successful and enjoys a wide and dedicated readership.

The difference may be that these newspapers make no secret of their biases—unlike American media outlets that claim to be objective and yet are clearly biased. For example, Ackerman said, when Fox News first went on the air in 1996, it adopted the slogan "Fair and Balanced," a motto that Ackerman and others found curious, given Fox's overtly conservative leanings. Ackerman said,

> *Some have suggested that Fox's conservative point of view and its Republican leanings render the network inherently unworthy as a news outlet. FAIR believes that view is misguided. The United States is unusual, perhaps even unique, in having a journalistic culture so fiercely wedded to the elusive notion of "objective" news ... In Great Britain, papers like the conservative* Times *of London and the left-leaning* Guardian *deliver consistently excellent coverage while making no secret of their respective points of view. There's nothing keeping American journalists from doing the same.*[1]

1. Seth Ackerman, "The Most Biased Name in News," FAIR, July 1, 2001. fair.org/extra/the-most-biased-name-in-news/

Cable news networks have frequently made claims of accuracy and credibility, but viewers have become more skeptical of such claims.

In 2002 when the study began, the average positive view of major news organizations was polled at 71 percent, while the negative view was only 30 percent. After only 10 years, the favorable rating had dropped to 56 percent and the negative view increased to 44 percent. The only source of news in the survey that did not experience a double-digit drop in credibility was local news sources.

This falling credibility is most obvious when looking at the ratings of the major cable news networks. At the beginning of the survey period, CNN had a 76 percent positive rating and Fox News had a 67 percent favorability rating. However, by 2012, the favorable rating for CNN and Fox News dropped by 18 percent for both organizations. Both cable sources saw their steepest decline in believability between 2010 and 2012. By comparison, local TV news sources have held strong with a 68 percent positive rating in 2002 and a 65 percent rating in 2012.

The survey also determined there is a strong relationship between someone's political affiliation and how believable they are likely to find a certain news source. Among Democrats, the perceived credibility of CNN only declined 8 percent, but with Republicans, it fell 32 percent. Fox News held strong with Republicans—only dropping 9 percent in positive ratings, but with Democrats it fell 30 percent. It seems that local TV news is the only sector where political affiliation does not play a strong role in determining its believability. Republican confidence in their local TV news only dropped 4 percent, while with Democrats, the drop was 2 percent.

Striking a balance between trusting and distrusting the press is becoming increasingly important. News outlets frequently report important information, even when it is slanted in one direction or another. Ignoring that information completely is foolish, especially since biased does not automatically mean false. A headline may be biased and attention-grabbing and the language used in the article may make the author's opinions clear, but it is possible to write a factually correct yet biased article.

Accepting everything the media says—especially when it comes from only one source—is also unwise. Being informed about current events is crucial because the decisions politicians make directly affect citizens; however, it can be a frustrating job to sort out the truth from the lies, which makes it tempting to sometimes give up on the news altogether. Nevertheless, it is a task that is well worth the effort, and finding the most unbiased sources possible can help people decide which way to vote and how to stand up for the issues that are important to them.

Some news sources are more biased than others. To remain informed, it is often best to seek information from many different sources.

NOTES

Introduction: History of Media Bias

1. Timothy Stanley, "Trump Is Right About Media Bias," CNN, April 30, 2017. www.cnn.com/2017/04/30/opinions/trump-is-right-about-media-bias-stanley/index.html.

Chapter 1: Where Does Media Bias Come From?

2. "Standards and Ethics," The *New York Times* Company, accessed October 4, 2017. www.nytco.com/who-we-are/culture/standards-and-ethics/.

3. Mike Argento, "Prez Column," National Society of Newspaper Columnists, October 26, 2008. www.columnists.com/2008/10/prez-column/.

4. Quoted in Jack Shafer, "Annenberg's Ticket Out of Hell," *Slate*, May 22, 2006. www.slate.com/id/2142154.

5. Tim Groseclose and Jeffrey Milyo, "A Measure of Media Bias," *Quarterly Journal of Economics*, November 2005, p. 1192.

6. Quoted in Melody Kramer, "Is Media Bias Really Rampant? Ask the Man Who Studies It for a Living," *Poynter*, October 24, 2016. www.poynter.org/news/media-bias-really-rampant-ask-man-who-studies-it-living.

7. Quoted in Groseclose and Milyo, "A Measure of Media Bias," p. 1206.

8. Groseclose and Milyo, "A Measure of Media Bias," p. 1206.

9. Kara Hackett, "A Reporter's Take on 'Liberal Media Bias,'" *Huffington Post*, May 23, 2017. www.huffingtonpost.com/entry/a-reporters-take-on-liberal-media-bias_us_591a5277e4b086d2d0d8d22b.

Chapter 2: Cable Entertainment and Fake News

10. Brian C. Anderson, *South Park Conservatives: The Revolt Against Liberal Media Bias*. Washington, D.C.: Regnery, 2005, pp. 51–52.

11. Kim Eisler, "Here Are the Top 50 Journalists," *Washingtonian*, March 1, 2001. www.washingtonian.com/2001/03/01/here-are-the-top-50-journalists/.

12. Mike Conway, Maria Elizabeth Grabe, and Kevin Grieves, "Villains, Victims and the Virtuous in Bill O'Reilly's 'No Spin Zone,'" *Journalism Studies*, 2007, p. 206.

13. Quoted in "Content Analysis of O'Reilly's Rhetoric Finds Spin to Be a 'Factor,'" Indiana University, May 2, 2007. newsinfo.iu.edu/news-archive/5535.html.

14. Brian Stelter, "Gotcha TV: Crews Stalk Bill O'Reilly's Targets," *New York Times*, April 16, 2009. www.nytimes.com/2009/04/16/arts/television/16ambush.html.

15. Quoted in Brian Stelter, "Gotcha TV: Crews Stalk Bill O'Reilly's Targets."

16. David Zurawik, "Rachel Maddow and the Power of Partisan Cable 'News,'" *Baltimore Sun*, October 28, 2008. www.baltimoresun.com/bs-mtblog-138807-rachel_maddow_the_power_of_par-story.html.

17. Quoted in John Timpane, "In the Obama Age, Fox News Finds the Right Stuff," Pop Matters, May 6, 2009. www.popmatters.com/article/92754-in-the-obama-age-fox-news-finds-the-right-stuff/.

18. Quoted in John Timpane, "In the Obama Age, Fox News Finds the Right Stuff."

19. "Obamacare vs. Affordable Care Act #2," YouTube video, 3:24, posted by Jimmy Kimmel Live, January 17, 2017. www.youtube.com/watch?v=N6m7pWEMPlA.

20. Steven Kull, Clay Ramsay, Stefan Subias, Evan Lewis, and Phillip Warf, "Misperceptions, the Media and the Iraq War," Program on International Policy Attitudes, University of Maryland, October 2, 2003. www.worldpublicopinion.org/pipa/articles/international_security_bt/102.php.

21. Steve Young, "The Way It Is—for Laughs," *Philadelphia Inquirer*, August 7, 2009, p. A-15.

22. "Alex Jones: Last Week Tonight with John Oliver (HBO)," YouTube video, 22:21, posted by LastWeekTonight, July 30, 2017. www.youtube.com/watch?v=WyGq6cjcc3Q.

23. "Alex Jones," YouTube video, posted by LastWeekTonight.

24. Quoted in Josh Constine, "Facebook Puts Link to 10 Tips for Spotting 'False News' Atop Feed," TechCrunch, April 6, 2017. techcrunch.com/2017/04/06/facebook-puts-link-to-10-tips-for-spotting-false-news-atop-feed/.

Chapter 3: The Internet and Journalism

25. Mary-Rose Papandrea, "Citizen Journalism and the Reporter's Privilege," *Minnesota Law Review*, February 16, 2007, p. 523.

26. Quoted in "The Conservative Critique and Rise of Conservative Media," *PBS Frontline: News War*, February 13, 2007. www.pbs.org/wgbh/pages/frontline/newswar/tags/conservative.html#4.

27. "Conservatism Today's 24 Best Conservative Blogs," Conservatism Today, August 6, 2008. www.conservatismtoday.com/my_weblog/2008/08/conservatism-to.html.

28. Quoted in "The Rise and Rise of Fake News," BBC, November 6, 2016. www.bbc.com/news/blogs-trending-37846860.

29. "The Rise and Rise of Fake News," BBC.

30. Quoted in "Welcome to the Blogosphere," PBS *NewsHour*, April 28, 2003. www.pbs.org/newshour/bb/media-jan-june03-blog_04-28/.

31. Quoted in "Welcome to the Blogosphere," PBS *NewsHour*.

32. Emma Woollacott, "The Viral Spread of Ebola Rumors," *Forbes*, October 9, 2014. www.forbes.com/sites/emmawoollacott/2014/10/09/the-viral-spread-of-ebola-rumors/#2526be0119d8.

33. Quoted in Papandrea, "Citizen Journalism and the Reporter's Privilege," p. 528.

34. Mitchell Stephens, "Beyond News: The Case for Wisdom Journalism," Joan Shorenstein Center on the Press, Politics and Public Policy, John F. Kennedy School of Government, Harvard University, 2009. www.hks.harvard.edu/presspol/publications/papers/discussion_papers/d53_stephens/pdf.

35. Sue Shellenbarger, "Most Students Don't Know When News Is Fake, Stanford Study Finds," *Wall Street Journal*, November 21, 2016. www.wsj.com/articles/most-students-dont-know-when-news-is-fake-stanford-study-finds-1479752576.

36. "Native Advertising: Last Week Tonight with John Oliver (HBO)," YouTube video, 11:22, posted by LastWeekTonight, August 3, 2014. www.youtube.com/watch?v=E_F5GxCwizc.

Chapter 4: Other Sources of Bias

37. Quoted in Jennifer Harper, "Gender Bias Did In Clinton?," *Washington Times*, June 6, 2008. www.washingtontimes.com/news/2008/jun/06/gender-bias-did-in-clinton.

38. Jessica Wakeman, "Misogyny's Greatest Hits," FAIR, June 1, 2008. fair.org/extra/misogynys-greatest-hits/.

39. Quoted in Jessica Lussenhop, "Presidential Debate 2016: Four Ways Gender Played a Role," BBC, September 27, 2016. www.bbc.com/news/election-us-2016-37481754.

40. Mary Bowerman, "Fox News' Brit Hume Under Fire for Saying Clinton 'Not Necessarily Attractive,'" *USA Today*, September 28, 2016. www.usatoday.com/story/news/politics/onpolitics/2016/09/27/fox-news-presidential-debate-hillary-clinton-appearance-brit-hume/91155602/.

41. Laura Italiano, "Evil Lesbian Mom Left Toddler to Die Slow Death: DA," *New York Post*, January 25, 2008. www.nypost.com/seven/01252008/news/regionalnews/evil_lesbian_mom_left_toddler_to_die_slo_736158.htm.

42. Snicks, "Best of the Worst: The GLAAD Anti-Gay Defamation List for 2008," Logo, January 7, 2009. www.newnownext.com/best-of-the-worst-the-glaad-anti-gay-defamation-list-for-2008/01/2009/.

43. "A Note to Our Readers," *Esquire*, April 17, 2009. www.esquire.com/the-side/note-to-our-readers-041309?src=digg.

44. Gabriel Arana, "Islamophobic Media Coverage Is Out of Control. It Needs to Stop," *Huffington Post*, November 18, 2015. www.huffingtonpost.com/entry/islamophobia-mainstream-media-paris-terrorist-attacks_us_564cb277e4b08c74b7339984.

45. Quoted in *The Black Press: Soldiers Without Swords*, PBS, 1998. www.pbs.org/blackpress/news_bios/index.html.

46. "Interview Transcripts: Frank Bolden," PBS, 1998. www.pbs.org/blackpress/film/transcripts/bolden.html.

47. Charles A. Simmons, *The African American Press: A History of News Coverage During National Crises, with Special Reference to Four Black Newspapers, 1827–1965*. Jefferson, NC: McFarland, 1998, p. 5.

48. Gillian B. White, "Where Are All the Minority Journalists?," *The Atlantic,* July 24, 2015. www.theatlantic.com/business/archive/2015/07/minorities-in-journalism/399461/.

49. White, "Where Are All the Minority Journalists?"

Chapter 5: Is All Media Biased?

50. "Adam Ruins Everything Corrects ITSELF!," YouTube video, 6:14, posted by CollegeHumor, August 30, 2017. www.youtube.com/watch?v=-ijl_kGG1eg.

51. "'It's Too Much LYING' Shep Smith LOSES COOL on Donald Trump's Lies—Fox News," YouTube video, 4:30, posted by USA News, March 9, 2017. www.youtube.com/watch?v=Spfbg8AW36U.

52. Quoted in Taylor Link, "Shepard Smith Debunks 'Fake News' That Puerto Rico Truck Drivers Are on Strike," *Salon*, October 4, 2017. www.salon.com/2017/10/04/shepard-smith-debunks-fake-news-that-puerto-rican-truck-drivers-are-on-strike/.

53. Quoted in Esther Scott, "Big Media Meets the Bloggers: Coverage of Trent Lott's Remarks at Strom Thurmond's Birthday Party," Kennedy School of Government, Harvard University, 2004. www.hks.harvard.edu/presspol/publications/case_studies/1731_0_scott.pdf.

54. Quoted in Scott, "Big Media Meets the Bloggers."

55. Quoted in Janet Waldman, "Out for the Count: Not Voting Helps Charlie Gibson with Quest to Be Fair," *Quinnipiac*, September 2008, p. 31.

56. Quoted in "Objectivity Tough Around Obama Fever," MSNBC, January 8, 2008. www.msnbc.msn.com/id/3032619/#22542498.

57. Brian Williams, "About Last Night," Daily Nightly, January 8, 2008. dailynightly.msnbc.msn.com/archive/2008/01/08/560859.aspx.

58. "Feministing," Media Bias/Fact Check, accessed September 19, 2017. mediabiasfactcheck.com/feministing/.

59. Dan Evon, "Fact Check: Did Ashley Judd Say She Wanted to Live in the Middle East 'Where Women Have More Rights?,'" Snopes, September 21, 2017. www.snopes.com/ashley-judd-middle-east-women-rights/.

Chapter 1:
Where Does Media Bias Come From?

1. Why are most journalists regarded as liberals?

2. How can columnists, editorial writers, and commentators avoid accusations of bias?

3. If a news source explains to its readers or viewers that their stories have a certain bias, is that bias still harmful?

Chapter 2:
Cable Entertainment and Fake News

1. In what ways have the hosts of cable news shows blurred the lines between news and entertainment?

2. Why is fake news dangerous?

3. Why have certain newspapers and cable news shows chosen to present information with a bias?

Chapter 3:
The Internet and Journalism

1. Why are news stories reported in blogs given less credibility than stories reported in newspapers and magazines?

2. How have blogs enabled readers to become active participants as news gatherers and commentators?

3. Why might an important news story be reported on a blog but not in regular news media?

Chapter 4:
Other Sources of Bias

1. What strategies do groups such as GLAAD use when they detect bias in the media?

2. How did African Americans overcome the refusal of the mainstream media to cover issues of importance to the black community?

3. Why do some media watchdog groups have a bias?

Chapter 5:
Is All Media Biased?

1. In what ways do some readers interpret news stories that prompt them to believe the media is biased?

2. How are accusations of bias causing the news media to lose credibility?

3. What resources can consumers of news tap to ensure they are receiving unbiased news coverage or at least know the biases of the media before they read the stories or tune in to the broadcasts?

4. If the news media has been losing credibility over the years, why have news shows' ratings been increasing?

ASNE

209 Reynolds Journalism Institute
Missouri School of Journalism
Columbia, MO 65211
(573) 882-2430
www.asne.org

> Formerly known as the American Society of News Editors, now known simply by its acronym, ASNE sets ethical standards for newspaper journalists, including rules regarding bias in their reporting. The organization defends freedom of the press and unbiased reporting.

Center for Media and Public Affairs

2338 S. Queen Street
Arlington, VA 22202
(202) 302-5523
www.cmpa.com

> The center is a nonprofit organization that performs studies of the media's impact on American society. Many of those studies have examined bias.

Federal Communications Commission (FCC)

445 12th St. SW
Washington, D.C. 20554
(888) 225-5322
www.fcc.gov

> The FCC regulates broadcasters in the United States. The organization's website includes many articles and other resources on the history and laws governing access to the airwaves.

Pew Research Center: Journalism and Media
1615 L St. NW, Suite 800
Washington, D.C. 20036
(202) 419-4300
www.journalism.org
> The Pew Research Center conducts studies on many topics, including journalism and the media.

Snopes
www.snopes.com
contact@teamsnopes.com
> This website conducts research to determine whether rumors circulated on the Internet are true or false. Users can submit stories they think should be fact-checked.

Books

Falk, Erika. *Women for President: Media Bias in Eight Campaigns.* Chicago, IL: University of Illinois Press, 2008.
> The author examines the ways gender bias by media dominated by male reporters and editors affected the campaigns of eight women who ran for president, starting with Victoria Woodhull in 1872 and ending with Carol Moseley Braun in 2004.

McChesney, Robert W. *Corporate Media and the Threat to Democracy.* New York, NY: Seven Stories Press, 2010.
> The author reviews the history of biased news in America and warns of a rising trend of corporate influences in U.S. politics.

Mooney, Carla. *Asking Questions About How the News Is Created.* Ann Arbor, MI: Cherry Lake Publishing, 2016.
> This volume explores the ways news outlets decide what news to report and how to report it.

Steele, Philip. *Race and Crime.* New York, NY: Crabtree Publishing, 2017.
> One major issue that is affected by media bias is the way race is reported on, especially when crimes are committed. This book examines the way race, crime, and police brutality are reported on around the world.

Websites

Accuracy in Media

www.aim.org

> Accuracy in Media (AIM) makes it clear that it searches for liberal bias in the media. Visitors to the group's website can find many examples of reporting that AIM feels are biased against conservatives.

Black Press USA

www.blackpressusa.com

> This group showcases the work of black journalists and is dedicated to telling the stories of the black community in the United States. It also features commentaries from world-renowned African American scholars, journalists, and activists.

Factitious

factitious.augamestudio.com/#/

> This game lets users test how skilled they are at spotting fake news.

Fairness & Accuracy in Reporting

www.fair.org

> This organization—dedicated to reporting on media bias with what some feel is a liberal spin— maintains a website that includes many resources about unbalanced reporting.

Media Bias/Fact Check

mediabiasfactcheck.com

> This website allows Internet users to check how biased and how factual various news outlets are.

INDEX

Lucian Vance is a freelance journalist living in San Francisco. In his free time, he plays a number of tabletop board games with his friends. He also enjoys taking long hikes and getting away from civilization sometimes. Lucian is currently working on his first science fiction graphic novel.